'Julie Macfarlane is presently Principal Lecturer in Law at Anglia College. She formerly worked with young people, first as a teacher and later as a social worker, and has lectured and campaigned on children's rights issues for a number of years. She lives in North London with her young daughter and her dog.'

Other titles in the *Sphere Rights Guides* series:

THE DIVORCE HANDBOOK Jenny Levin
THE MOBILE HOMES HANDBOOK Linda Pearce
THE RACE DISCRIMINATION HANDBOOK Harjit Grewal
THE HOMELESS PERSONS HANDBOOK Andrew Arden
THE DISABLED PERSONS HANDBOOK Jan Luba
THE PRIVATE TENANTS HANDBOOK Andrew Arden
THE PUBLIC TENANTS HANDBOOK Andrew Arden
THE DISABLED PERSONS HANDBOOK Jan Luba
THE SEX DISCRIMINATION HANDBOOK Harjit Grewal
THE OWNER-OCCUPIER HANDBOOK Jan Luba
THE SINGLE PARENTS HANDBOOK Jenny Levin and
    Frances Logan
THE LAWYER-CLIENT HANDBOOK Ole Hansen
THE TIED ACCOMMODATION HANDBOOK Jenny Levin

SPHERE RIGHTS GUIDES
Series Editor: Andrew Arden

THE CHILDREN'S RIGHTS HANDBOOK

JULIE MACFARLANE

SPHERE REFERENCE

A SPHERE BOOK

First published in Great Britain
by Sphere Books Ltd 1990

Copyright © Julie Macfarlane 1990

Typeset in Plantin by Leaper & Gard Ltd, Bristol, England
Reproduced, printed and bound in Great Britain by
The Guernsey Press

ISBN 0-7474-0214-0

Sphere Books Ltd
A Division of
Macdonald & Co (Publishers) Ltd
Orbit House, 1 New Fetter Lane, London EC4A 1AR
A Member of Maxwell Pergamon Publishing Corporation

To Sibyl, Aisling and Fíona,
hoping that you will always stand up for your rights.

Acknowledgements

In order to produce a book such as this which deals with a broad canvas of issues relating to children's rights, I have been advised and encouraged by many people. In particular I would like to thank the following for their comments on the text: Penny Muir; Ben Muir; Rachel Hodgkin of the Childrens Legal Centre; Lindsey Squire and Richard Edwards at Anglia Law School; Damhnait Rumney; Debbie Donovan and Brenda Macfarlane. Also Jane Franklin for providing the childcare which freed me to write this book; my parents for the supplementary childcare which enabled me to finish it; and Nita Lloyd and Pat Bower at the Anglia Law School for their patience with me while I endlessly printed out material and got under their feet.

Julie Macfarlane
London December 1989

Publisher's Note

The Law can change at short notice. This book describes the law relating to children's rights as at 31st January 1990. You should always check if what it says is still correct.

Contents

Introduction   **01**

1: Young People and Money, Work and Housing 05

A. SPENDING MONEY AND OWNING PROPERTY – HOW THE LAW
REGARDS YOUNG PEOPLE

Is there any way I can borrow money before I reach 18?
At what age can I open a bank (building society, post
   office) account?
At what age can I buy shares in a public company?
At what age can I become a tenant by taking on a lease?

B. SOURCES OF INCOME FOR CHILDREN AND YOUNG PEOPLE

1. Paid Work
At what age can I be employed in paid work?
Is there any type of work I may not do?
What about working in my family's business?
Will I have to pay tax and national insurance
   contributions on my earnings?
Is there a minimum wage for young people under 18?
What is the Youth Training Scheme?

2. Social Security Payments
What benefits can my parents claim on my behalf?
If I leave school at 16 but carry on living at home, am I
   entitled to receive any benefits in my own right?
Will I be entitled to any social security benefits if I move
   away from home?
I am on a YTS course, but I am thinking of leaving. Will I
   qualify for unemployment benefit?

I am a student studying on a further/higher education
    course. Am I entitled to any social security benefits?
I am a single parent under 18. What benefits am I entitled
    to claim?
My child is in care but visits me regularly at the weekends.
    Am I entitled to claim any benefits on his behalf?
How do I appeal against a decision not to grant me
    benefit?

2: The Right To An Education 17

A. CHOICE OF SCHOOLING

Does the State have any legal duty to provide schooling
    for the under-fives?
Is it true that it is the parents who are responsible for
    ensuring that their children receive an education?
What if my child refuses to attend school?
Can I educate my child at home if I want to?
There are several schools nearby where we live. Can I
    choose which one I send my children to?
How would I appeal against the education authority's
    decision on my choice of school?
One of our local schools is described as 'voluntary-aided'.
    What does this mean?
What difference will it make if my child's school 'opts out'
    of local authority control?

B. OTHER CONSIDERATIONS AFFECTING SCHOOL CHOICE

I am anxious about my son taking part in sports such as
    rugby. What liability, if any, does the school have if he is
    injured?
I object to my children taking part in a Christian or other
    form of religious assembly at school. What can I do
    about it?

Contents

My child has special religious and dietary requirements
which I want him to observe during the school day. Can
I ask his school to make arrangements for this?

Is the education authority obliged to provide my child with
free school meals or milk?

Is my child entitled to free medical and dental checks at
school?

What obligations do schools have to prevent sex or race
discrimination?

C. THE SCHOOL CURRICULUM

What will the 'National Curriculum' mean for my child's
schooling?

I don't like the way that sex education is taught at my
child's school. What can I do about it?

I heard that under the new law schools are allowed to
charge for some services. Is this right and what sort of
things might I be charged for?

D. DISCIPLINE

Who has final authority in deciding what standards of
discipline are to be applied in each school?

Are the teachers at my child's school entitled to use
corporal punishment (e.g. cane, slap with a ruler)?

My son has come home with a letter saying that he is
suspended from attending school for one week because
of bad behaviour. On what grounds is the school
allowed to suspend him, and can we appeal?

My son's school has written to me to say that they are
excluding him until he gets his hair cut and wears the
correct school uniform. Can they exclude him from the
school on these grounds and must we comply if he is to
return to this school?

My daughter's school has written to me saying that they

intend to expel her for bad behaviour. On what grounds are they entitled to expel her?

Am I entitled to access to my child's school records? Can I appeal against anything that is written there if I feel that it is unfair?

I cannot afford to buy my child's school uniform. The school says that they won't accept him without the uniform. What can I do?

E. SPECIAL EDUCATION

I think that my son may have learning difficulties and I would like him to be professionally assessed. What are the local education authority's duties?

The education authority has written to me to say that they want to carry out an assessment of my son's 'special educational needs', but I feel that he is happy in his present school and that this would be disruptive and unnecessary. Can I object to the assessment being carried out?

I don't want my child to go to a 'special school' but to a mainstream school with special classes for 'slow learners'. Do I have the right to demand this?

Our local school is threatened with closure because of falling rolls. How can we fight this?

3: Children and the Criminal Justice System   **39**

At what age does a child become liable to prosecution under the criminal law?

Up to what age is a young person classified as a 'juvenile offender'?

Are parents ever liable on behalf of their children for the crimes they commit?

Are there any special defences open to children?

Contents

A. YOUNG PEOPLE AND THE POLICE

Can the police insist on carrying out a search in the street on a child or a young person?

Do I have to give the police my name and address if they stop me in the street and ask me who I am?

Can the police take away anything they find if they stop and search me in the street?

Can I be questioned by the police at school?

Can the police ask a juvenile to go to the police station to be questioned?

What is the difference between 'assisting with inquiries' and being arrested?

When I start being questioned, do I have to answer questions if I don't want to, or think that it is better if I don't?

Do I have the right to phone my parents, friend, social worker or a solicitor?

What happens if I don't know any solicitors, and neither do my parents?

Will I have to pay the solicitor?

Can the police keep me in the police station overnight?

For how long can I be questioned without a break?

Can the police insist on taking a child's fingerprints?

Can the police insist on carrying out a body search at a police station on a child or young person?

What happens if I am held and questioned in the police station for eight hours and then released without charge?

After being arrested and questioned, the police have sent me home on 'police bail' and say that I must report back in two weeks' time. What does this mean will happen to me? Will I have to go to court?

I have been charged by the police after questioning and sent home. What happens next?

Are the police allowed to stop me going home after I have been charged?

On what grounds is bail awarded and what conditions
    might be attached?
Under what circumstances can a juvenile be remanded to
    a remand centre or prison?

B. YOUNG PEOPLE AND THE CRIMINAL COURTS

Which court hears criminal charges brought against a
    juvenile?
Who sits in the juvenile court?
Is the juvenile court hearing open to the public?
Can I have my own solicitor?
How will I pay for the solicitor?
What role does the juvenile court welfare officer play?
What is the 'social inquiry' report?
Will I have the chance to see the social inquiry report
    myself?
Will I have to answer questions in court?
Can I appeal if I am found guilty?

C. CUSTODIAL SENTENCES

Does the juvenile court have the power to give me a
    custodial sentence?
How long can I be sentenced to serve?
Can a juvenile be sentenced to serve time in an adult
    prison or a remand centre?
What does it mean if a court sentences a young person to
    be 'detained at Her Majesty's pleasure'?

D. NON-CUSTODIAL SENTENCES

1. Attendance Centre Orders

2. Probation/Supervision Orders

I have been put on probation for a year. What does this
    mean?

Contents

Can I choose who I have as my probation officer?
What happens if I break the terms of my probation?

3. *Fines*
If I am fined by the court, will I have to pay it all at once?
What happens if I don't pay?

4. *Community Service Orders*
What sort of work does community service involve?
Do I have to do community service if I don't want to?
What happens if I don't carry out the work programme I
    have been assigned?

5. *Binding Over to Keep the Peace*

**4: Parental Custody and
Access to Children**   **59**

What is the meaning of 'custody'?
What principles do the courts apply in resolving disputes
    over who should have custody?
What is meant by 'care and control'? Is it the same as
    custody?
What are 'joint custody' orders?
What changes will the new law in the Children Act make?
In what circumstances is it anticipated that 'specific
    issue' and 'prohibited steps' orders will be made?
I am prepared for my ex-wife to stay in our family home
    and for the children to live with her there. However, I
    am paying maintenance and I feel that I should still
    have a say in how the children are brought up. Does
    paying maintenance give me this right?
What can I do to ensure that I continue to have a say in
    how my children grow up?
I am prepared for my ex-wife to have custody of our three
    children but I still want to be able to see them on a
    regular basis. What steps should I take to ensure this?

I am worried that my ex-husband will insist on our son going to his old school. I would much rather he attended the local school with his friends. Can I insist on this?

My child was born as a result of my relationship with my co-habitee, but that relationship is now over. What is my position on custody of my child?

Does it make any difference that my boyfriend's name is on the child's birth certificate?

I am the father of my ex-girlfriend's child and want to see my child regularly and maybe have him to stay with me when he is older. My ex-girlfriend will not co-operate with this. What can I do to ensure that I can have access?

My ex-girlfriend had our baby a year ago and is living alone with him in a hostel. I don't believe that she can care for him properly and I want to take over his upbringing myself. What rights do I have?

My boyfriend and I have been living together for three years and we have recently had a child. What steps can we take to give my boyfriend a legal status in relation to our child?

How do rights to custody and access affect the payment of maintenance for a child?

Do the procedures of applying for maintenance for a child born outside marriage differ from applications for maintenance payments towards keeping children of a marriage?

5: Local Authority Responsibilities for Children, Young People and Families   **73**

What types of assistance can children and young people in trouble expect from the local authority for the area in which they live?

Contents

How do I find out which local authority has responsibility for me?

Up to what age do local authorities have legal responsibilities towards children and young people living in their area?

Are there any other qualifications for assistance?

A. QUESTIONS FOR PARENTS

My children live at home with me and I wouldn't want them taken into care, even on a temporary basis. However, I do feel that I need some outside support in order to cope. What can the local authority do to help?

Many of my family's problems are money-related. Can the local authority do anything to help?

How can I persuade the local authority social worker that my family should qualify for family services and/or financial assistance?

I don't want my children taken into care permanently, but I cannot look after them properly at the moment. Can the local authority do anything to help?

Can I make private fostering arrangements for my child to see us through a difficult period?

Can I be asked to contribute towards the cost of my child's upkeep whilst he is in care?

What sort of rights does this voluntary arrangement give social workers and foster parents to make decisions about my child whilst he is in their care?

What about emergencies?

How can I ensure that my child's case is regularly reviewed by the social workers responsible?

Will I be consulted about the review?

Is there any formal mechanism for making a complaint to the local authority about any aspects of their handling of my child's case?

What happens when I decide that I am ready to cope with
my child returning home to live with me?

B. QUESTIONS FOR CHILDREN AND YOUNG PEOPLE

Where will I live while I am in voluntary care?
Will I carry on going to the same school?
How often will I see my parents?
I have been told by my social worker that there is going to
be a 'case conference' about me. What does this mean?
Can I go to the case conference?
What if I decide that I want to go home to my own family?
Does the council have any duty to provide me with
housing if I am homeless?

6: Going Into Care 91

What does the law mean when it talks about 'taking a
child into care'?
What sort of arguments must the social workers make to
persuade the magistrates (or presently the social services
committee) that a child would be better off in full care?
What sort of 'proof' do the magistrates look for before
making an order?

A. QUESTIONS FOR PARENTS

Will I receive an official notice from the local authority of
its intention to take my child into full care?
Can I have a solicitor to represent me in court?
My child is too young to express an opinion over where
or with whom she wants to live. Does this give me the
right to speak on her behalf?
My child has said that he doesn't want to live with me any
more and he has told the social worker this too. Does
this mean that I cannot argue against the local
authority in court?

Who else can talk to the court on my behalf – for example,
    can my child's grandmother or aunt or a family friend
    or neighbour tell the court that my child is best left at
    home with me?

What sort of questions will the magistrates ask me in
    court?

On what basis will the magistrates make up their minds?

What sort of orders can the magistrates make?

Can we appeal against the making of a care order?

If my child is taken into full care, where will he live?

Will I have any say in my child's life once he is in full care?

Will I be able to visit my child?

The social worker has told me that my child's foster
    parents want to adopt him. Do I have to agree?

My home situation has completely changed since my child
    went into care. Can I now get the care order lifted in
    order that he can come home and live with me?

B. QUESTIONS FOR CHILDREN AND YOUNG PEOPLE

Will I be asked to appear in court and what sort of
    questions will I be asked?

Will I have my own solicitor, or anyone else, to explain to
    the court how I feel?

Will I be allowed to remain in court when other people (my
    parents, for example) are being questioned?

Will I be allowed to see the reports my social
    worker/probation officer/education social
    worker/guardian *ad litem* write for the magistrate?

If I am taken into full care, will I be allowed to decide
    where I live?

What if I don't like the children's home or foster home my
    social worker finds for me?

What if I don't want my parents to visit me, or if I want my
    parents to visit me more often?

What happens in relation to pocket-money and buying
    clothes and other things I need?

I shall be 18 soon and my care order will lapse. I can't
  return home. Will the local authority help me to find
  somewhere to live?
What sort of advice and assistance can I expect?
How can local authorities act to protect children in
  emergency situations at home?

7: Emergency Protection for Children in Danger 109

How can local authorities act to protect children in an
  'emergency'?
How does the local authority obtain the legal right to
  remove from their homes children believed to be in
  danger?
Does the law give any special powers to the police to
  intervene in cases of suspected abuse?
How in practice will the new law enforce emergency
  provisions for the removal of children where the family
  refuse to allow social workers into the home?
Am I obliged to allow my child to be examined by a doctor
  before the emergency order is made?
How long can an emergency order last?
Who does the law regard as exercising parental rights once
  an emergency order is made?
Where will my child be accommodated if an emergency
  order has been made?
Will I be allowed to visit my child after he has been taken
  away under an emergency order?
Once an emergency order has been made, what happens
  next?
I have read of children being removed from their parents
  in emergencies after being made 'wards of court'. What
  does this mean?
I have found out that a member of my household has been
  abusing my child, who has been removed under an
  emergency order. The social worker has told me that

my child cannot come home until this person has left.
What can I do?

What sort of follow-up care such as personal counselling is
available for family members after abuse has been
discovered?

8: Adoption   123

What is the effect of an adoption order?
On what grounds will the court agree to making an
adoption order?

A. QUESTIONS FOR PROSPECTIVE ADOPTERS

Who can be adopted?
Who can adopt?
But surely not just anyone can adopt?
What about adoptions by relatives of the child?
What about adoptions by step-parents?
Who can arrange an adoption?
I have been fostering a child for the past five years whom I
now want to adopt. How do I go about this and might
the child be removed in the meantime if his mother
objects?
Will I have to hire a solicitor?
Where will the adoption hearing take place?
What alternative orders might the court make if it is not
convinced that adoption is appropriate at this time?
I am not sure that I am ready to consider adoption, but I
would like to feel more secure about the future of our
foster child in our family. What could I do?
I took a short-term foster child into my home last year
whom I would now like to adopt. My social worker tells
me that he is already 'freed for adoption'. What does
this mean?

B. QUESTIONS FOR NATURAL PARENTS

My child has been in the full care of the local authority for
  some years now. Can the social workers go ahead and
  arrange for his adoption without my permission?
What if I gave my consent when adoption was first
  suggested, but have now changed my mind?
The social worker has asked me to agree to 'freeing' my
  child for adoption. What does this mean?
If my child is adopted, will I be able to continue to see him?
I am the father of my ex-girlfriend's child. She is
  intending to place the baby for adoption. Can I oppose
  this?

C. QUESTIONS FOR ADOPTED CHILDREN

What difference will my views make on whether the
  adoption goes ahead?
I am adopted and my adoptive parents have other children
  of their own living at home. Are they my brothers and
  sisters?
Can I find out who my natural parents are?

**9: Other Issues Affecting Children and Young
People**   **139**

1. Medical Treatment
At what age can I give my consent to medical treatment?
What if I am under 16?
Can I get contraceptive advice or treatment, or an
  abortion without my parents' consent and without them
  having to know?
What about other sorts of medical treatment, like being
  prescribed a drug substitute to break my heroin
  addiction?

2. *Young People and Sexuality*
My boyfriend and I have been having sexual intercourse
    together since I was 14. Does this mean that he could be
    prosecuted?
My friend says that if I have intercourse under age with
    my boyfriend I will be taken into care. Is this true?
What about boys?
Are sexual relations between members of the same family
    (for example a father with his daughter or son) against
    the law?

3. *Parental Physical Punishment*

4. *Running Away From Home*

5. *Driving*

6. *Drinking*

10: Getting Legal Advice and Representation   147
Useful addresses

Introduction

Children's rights have in the past been largely described in terms of parents' rights. For example, children were regarded as the 'property' of their parents in law well into this century, giving parents the right of control over all aspects of their children's upbringing. Parents have been permitted by the law to treat their children in ways (for example, abducting and imprisoning them, or physically punishing them) which would have been considered by the law to be criminal behaviour in any other context. Over the past fifteen years, the rights of children as individuals have begun to be separated from those of their parents and this is reflected in new laws passed by Parliament and the decisions made in the courts.

Many people have read something about the decision of the House of Lords in the case brought by Mrs Gillick, the mother who wanted to prevent her daughters, and any other girl under 16, from receiving contraceptive advice or treatment from a doctor without her parent's knowledge and permission. The decision of the Law Lords that a parent did not have the automatic legal right to prevent his or her children from seeing a doctor in confidence and that the maturity and circumstances of the individual was a matter for the discretion of the doctor in each case was a milestone in the developing history of independent rights for children and young people.

In less dramatic ways also the law has been changing. Much publicized cases of child abuse and child poverty have increased public awareness of the need for public or State intervention in families on behalf of children who are suffering or in need. The increase in divorce has turned our attention to the hundreds of thousands of children who are affected by the break-up of their parents' marriages. To resolve disputes over a child's uncertain future, the principle of 'the best interests of the child' has been developed in the courts as a basis for reaching a decision and now, wherever possible, the wishes of the child must be taken into account. A good illustration of this is that access to a child by a parent where the parent's marriage or relationship has broken down is now seen first and foremost as the right of the child – where it is in his or her 'best interests' – rather than the automatic right of the parent seeking access.

Many questions and problems remain. Cases such as Gillick establish new approaches to age-old dilemmas about parental authority. Increasingly the law emphasizes parental responsibilities, or duties, rather than rights, and this approach is illustrated in the new law in the Children Act 1989, described in this book.

Gradually, the distinctive nature of the law relating to children, or the law which treats children differently from adults, has grown in volume and significance. In this book these areas are dealt with in turn. In each chapter, the questions which are answered include some I might expect a parent to ask, some I would expect a child to ask, and some I might anticipate from a social worker or other child agency worker.

A note on the scope of this book

This book covers the law in England and Wales. Scotland and Northern Ireland have separate legal systems and sometimes the law relating to children is different there. In England and Wales, the Children Act 1989 will bring about many changes in law and practice and these have been included. However, in many areas the new law will not come into force for a year or more, and therefore the law at present in force – soon to be the old law – is also described.

A note on courts

Many of the matters which concern children (for example, care proceedings and juvenile crime) are dealt with by a special court created for the purpose, known as the juvenile court. This is usually located in part of a magistrates court building. In other areas the consideration of cases involving children or young people takes place alongside adults in the same court system.

A note on terminology

There is no consistent legal definition of the word 'child'. In some areas the law sees a 'child' as someone less than 10 years old; in others 14 years old; in others 16 or 18 and so on. Each chapter of this book deals with a particular aspect of the law as it affects children and young people; each has its own definition of what is considered to be a child.

The law regards the married parents of a child as 'parents'. Where a child is born as a result of a non-marital relationship, the law in the first instance (see also Chapter 4) only recognizes the mother of the child as 'parent'. Any individual who becomes a child's 'guardian' is recognized by the law in most respects as a 'parent' of that child in law.

1: Young People and Money, Work and Housing

A. SPENDING MONEY AND OWNING PROPERTY – HOW THE LAW REGARDS YOUNG PEOPLE

When money and/or property is owned by a young person under the age of 18, the law applies a different set of rules than those which apply to someone over the age of 18. The most important difference is that the law regards anyone under 18 as lacking the 'capacity' to enter into a contract or any agreement for goods or credit. What this means in theory is that any purchase by a young person under 18 of anything other than 'necessaries' (see below), with money or on credit, is unenforceable in the eyes of the law. What this means in practice is that young people under 18 generally cannot take out credit, loan or hire purchase agreements.

The only exception is where the contract is for the purchase of 'necessaries'. Basically this amounts to items necessary for daily life rather than 'luxury' items (for example, a set of fancy waistcoats has been held to be 'necessary' only to an Oxford undergraduate – and probably only when this case was decided in the last century). The exception is so narrow that in practice it is disregarded, so that, unless the trader will accept an adult guarantor (see below) and you can provide one, you cannot contract to buy any goods under the age of 18 except with cash.

Is there any way I can borrow money before I reach 18?

The only circumstance in which you can take out credit, a loan or hire purchase agreement before you are 18 is if an adult acts as a guarantor for you. This means in effect that if you default on the agreement, or if you do not have sufficient money in your bank account to cover the cheque, the debt – which cannot be enforced against you under 18 – can be enforced against the adult. This is a considerable responsibility for anyone to undertake on your behalf. There is, in any case, no need for a hire purchase, credit card company or bank even to offer you the possibility of an agreement backed by a guarantor (assuming that you can find one; sometimes a parent or guardian is stipulated). Different businesses have their own policies on this.

At what age can I open a bank (building society, post office) account?

This depends upon the bank or building society. For example, girobank allows young people to open accounts at 15 with an adult guarantor (see below). However, the rule that you are not able to contract for the purchase of goods (other than 'necessaries'; see above) until you are 18 means that, although you can keep money in a bank or building society or post office giro account, and at a certain age (specified by the bank or building society but usually around 12) you can sign out your own money in cash, you cannot write cheques since these are a promise to pay money; as a minor you don't have the 'capacity' to promise this (see above). For the same reason, you are not entitled to a cheque card guaranteeing payment on your cheques until you reach 18. Similarly, any agreement for a loan from your bank or building society cannot be enforced in law.

At what age can I buy shares in a public company?

The purchase of shares by a young person under 18 is one of several special exceptions to the general rule that an infant does not have the capacity to make contracts. You can buy shares before the age of 18 and you will then be bound to any terms (for example, paying for the shares) which are imposed on any adult who buys shares in that company. You are entitled, though, to 'repudiate' the contract, that is to change your mind and back out, at any time before you are 18. You will still have to pay what is already owed on the shares by this time but can avoid any future liability.

At what age can I become a tenant by taking on a lease?

If you are under the age of 18 you cannot own property or hold a 'legal interest' in property. Similarly, you cannot be a legal tenant in the full sense of taking on all future legal liabilities which may flow from the tenancy. In the same way as the purchase of shares, signing an agreement to take on a lease binds you to its terms (including payment of rent) until the agreement is repudiated, which theoretically may be done at any time while you are under 18. Like shares (above), you are liable only for payments due before the date of repudiation. Just like an adult you are expected to keep to any other terms of the agreement, for example to maintain the property in good order, for as long as the agreement is in effect – that is unless and until you repudiate it.

The same applies to an agreement to grant a contractual 'licence' to live in a property and pay rent.

Despite the legal difficulties involved in granting tenancies to young people under the age of 18, the Association of Metropolitan Authorities recommends that councils regard anyone over the age of 16 as a genuine housing applicant. Most local authorities have arrangements for letting to young people under 18, usually requiring an adult guarantor (sometimes the authority's Social Services Department will act as guarantor).

For details of the legal responsibilities of local authorities to accommodate young people under 18, see Chapter 6.

B. SOURCES OF INCOME FOR CHILDREN AND YOUNG PEOPLE

Most children and young people have three possible sources of income: from their families, from their own paid work, or from social security benefits which may be payable either to them or to their families on their behalf.

Maintenance payments for children where a family does not live together are dealt with in Chapter 4. Income for young people from paid work and from social security benefits are discussed below.

1. Paid Work

The rule that anyone under 18 does not have the 'capacity' (see above) to make a legal contract applies in principle to contracts with employers also. Contracts for the employment of young people under 18 will be enforceable if they are fair and generally for the benefit of the young person. This means that the courts still have a discretion to strike down a contract of employment if its terms are regarded as harsh – for example if the wages are very low and the hours very long. In general this rule allows for the legal recognition of contracts of employment for young people under 18.

At what age can I be employed in paid work?
13. Under 13 the law does not allow an employer to contract with a child for paid work. From 13 you may work up to two hours a day (outside school hours) during term time. This rule is relaxed at 16.

Is there any type of work I may not do?
Legislation prevents the employment of anyone under 16
in a factory, underground in a mine or on a ship. You
cannot work in a bar or other licensed premises until you
are 18.

What about working in my family's business?
Strictly speaking, the law makes no distinction between
young people employed in a family business and young
people employed anywhere else. However, in practice
these rules are enforced by local authorities and local
authorities may make by-laws permitting the employment
of young people in a family business under specified
circumstances. You could ask at your town hall.

**Will I have to pay tax and national insurance
contributions on my earnings?**
Yes, in exactly the same way as an adult. The first £2785
(1990/91 rates) you earn in any one tax year (April to
April) is not taxed.

**Is there a minimum wage for young people under
18?**
No. There is no minimum wage protection for anyone
under the age of 21.

What is the Youth Training Scheme?
The Government sponsors Youth Training Scheme
places for every school leaver, no matter what your
qualifications. If you do not take up the offer of a YTS
place and have no other source of income, you will not be
able to claim income support (see below).

The scheme involves either one or two year placements
with an employer. If you enter a one year scheme, you
will be paid £29.50 a week for the first three months, and
£35 a week for the remaining nine (1989/90 rates). You

can expect to work up to 40 hours a week (but no more) and have seven weeks 'off-the-job' training, probably in a local technical college. If you enter a two year scheme, you will be paid at the lower rate (at present £29.50 a week) for the first year and £35 a week for the second year. You will not be entitled to any additional benefit from income support to supplement your wages but you may be entitled to housing benefit if you are living away from home.

At the beginning of your YTS placement you should be given a Training Agreement, outlining the sort of training you will receive over the next one to two years. You should discuss this with your supervisor, and if any of the terms of the Agreement are subsequently broken you should take the matter up with him or her.

As a trainee, you are entitled to at least 1.5 days a month paid holiday and public and bank holidays in addition. You should also be given time off to attend interviews elsewhere. In some important respects you do not have the same legal rights as a trainee as other workers. For example, you do not have the right to any period of notice, nor to a written statement of reasons for dismissing you. You are entitled to join the workplace trade union.

2. Social Security Payments

There are three kinds of social security payment which relate to children and young people. First, there are those payments which are made to the parent or guardian in respect of the child; these are child benefit, single parent benefit and family credit (formerly family income supplement or FIS). Second, payments can be made direct to a young person over 16 who has left school and has no income; this is income support or grants from the social fund. Third, payments may be made to a third party such as a landlord on behalf of the young person; for example housing benefit.

Please note that all figures given below for benefits are correct as of April 1990, but are subject to change.

What benefits can my parents claim on my behalf?

Child benefit (£7.25 a week) may be claimed for you by your parent or guardian until you are 16 years old. If you are in full-time education (more than 12 hours a week) it may be claimed for you until you are 19. Once you take up a job (working more than 24 hours a week) or a place on a Youth Training Scheme, it will no longer be payable.

If you live with one parent only and he or she is either single or separated, and not living with anyone else, he or she may also claim one-parent benefit. This is £5.60 a week. It is paid regardless of income, in the same way as child benefit.

Family credit is also available to some families with children. To qualify there must be at least one child under the age of 16 (or 19 if still in full-time education), and one of the adults in the household (your mother, your father, or the common law partner of either your mother or father) must work for at least 24 hours a week and earn below a certain amount (depending upon how many people that salary must support). For details you can look at leaflet FB27 produced by the Department of Social Security which should be available at your local post office.

If I leave school at 16 but carry on living at home, am I entitled to receive any benefits in my own right?

If you are between 16 and 18 and living at home with your parents, you do not qualify for income support

(£20.80 a week rising to £27.40 when you become 18) unless you can show 'severe circumstances' or one or more of a number of prescribed conditions. Generally speaking it is very unlikely that you will be able to claim income support while you remain living at home. However, it is by no means automatic that you will qualify even if you move away from home (see below).

If you are living at home, the only 'prescribed conditions' that may apply to you are that you are in poor health or have some other physical or mental handicap or illness which prevents you from working for the next 12 months. You will not qualify for income support if you are offered, but turn down, a place on a Youth Training Scheme unless you can show illness or some other form of incapacity as described above. To show incapacity you will need medical evidence from your doctor and any other specialist who has treated you. If you can produce such evidence you can expect a decision on whether you qualify for income support within 24 hours. You may appeal against an unfavourable decision (see below).

Whether or not you live in your parents' home, you may also claim if you have sole responsibility for a child which prevents you from working. If you have a child to look after you will also be able to claim child benefit and, if you are unmarried, single parent benefit also.

You may qualify for unemployment benefit if you have worked in the past and made sufficient contributions through your pay packet to the National Insurance Scheme. This is unaffected by whether or not you are still living at home. However, it is very unlikely that you will have reached the required level of past contributions by the age of 16 or 17. In any case, you will be expected to take up a place on a Youth Training Scheme (see above).

Will I be entitled to any social security benefits if I move away from home?

It is not the case simply by moving out of the family home that you make yourself eligible for income support (the away-from-home weekly rate for 16–18 year olds is £27.40). You will qualify under the 'prescribed conditions' only if you are genuinely homeless and you must show a good reason why you are not living at home, for example overcrowding (strictly defined) or that you are estranged from your parents. Young people unable to live at home because of fear of physical or sexual abuse also qualify for support. So do young people who have lived in care for the previous two years (see Chapter 6).

If you are living away from home you may also qualify for housing benefit towards your rent or payment for board and lodgings. This is paid by local authorities, but it is determined by regulations if you are also in receipt of income support which restrict the period of time you can claim (the 'initial period') while you live in any one place. Generally speaking, you can claim for just two weeks in a seaside town, four weeks in most major towns and cities, and for up to six weeks maximum elsewhere. After the 'initial period' has expired, you must move on to another area in order to make a fresh claim.

You may also apply for a special payment for a specified purpose under the social fund. This will take the form of a loan (repayable over a maximum of 78 weeks). There are a number of specially prescribed circumstances in which social fund payments may be made. Most of these include the requirement that the applicant is on income support. Regulations for the administration of the social fund make young people who cannot live at home for emotional or practical reasons a priority and these are the same young people who may qualify for income support under the 'prescribed conditions' (see above). Otherwise, payment of a 'crisis loan' may be made, where the applicant is not on income support, in circumstances of extreme hardship. This decision is made by the benefit office you apply to but can in certain circumstances be, appealed against (see below).

I am on a YTS course, but I am thinking of leaving. Will I qualify for unemployment benefit?

If you are over 18, you will be entitled to unemployment benefit once you have finished your YTS placement. You should note that, since the Social Security Act 1989 became law, all unemployment benefit claimants are now required to prove that they are 'actively seeking work' in order to continue to receive benefit.

If you leave YTS voluntarily and without 'good reason' or lose your place through 'misconduct' (for example, persistent lateness or unauthorized time off) you will be disqualified from claiming for up to 26 weeks. If you are under 18 it is unlikely that you will qualify for unemployment benefit anyway since you will not have made enough contributions.

You will be subject to the conditions for right to claim income support described above.

If you have worked since leaving school or are between YTS placements you may be entitled to a 'bridging allowance' (presently £15 a week) for up to eight weeks. You will not get this if you have left your previous placement without 'good reason'.

I am a student studying on a further/higher education course. Am I entitled to any social security benefits?

If you fall within the 'prescribed conditions' (see above) you will be entitled to claim income support during any vacation period not covered by your grant (if you are receiving one). On the same principle, if you are the recipient of a student loan after 1990 you will only be entitled to claim during those periods which you can show your loan was not designed to cover.

You may be able to claim housing benefit in term time, but only if you are living in private accommodation (and not with your parents), and not if you live in accommodation provided by the college, such as a hall of residence.

I am a single parent under 18. What benefits am I entitled to claim?

You can claim child benefit and single parent benefit (above). Since you have responsibility for a child you may also be able to claim income support since this is one of the 'prescribed conditions' (see above). However, note that you may lose your right to claim income support and your entitlement to single parent benefit if you live with a boyfriend.

My child is in care but visits me regularly at the weekends. Am I entitled to claim any benefits on his behalf?

The general rule is that payment of both child benefit and one-parent benefit stops after your child has been in care for eight weeks. You can continue to claim child benefit and one-parent benefit if you can show that your child visits you 'reasonably often'. You may similarly qualify for family credit. You may also be able to claim travelling expenses if you travel to visit your child while he or she is in care.

How do I appeal against a decision not to grant me benefit?

Most decisions by your local benefits office may be referred for appeal to an adjudication officer within three months of you being notified of the original decision. The adjudication officer is obliged to return a decision on your appeal within 14 days. If this decision also goes against you, you may take your case to the Social Security Appeal Tribunal for a full hearing.

You can find out how to appeal to the Social Security Appeal Tribunal from your local Citizens' Advice Bureau or Law Centre. There is a tribunal in each county or city area which hears all cases arising in that district, so you should not have to travel far for a hearing. You can expect to receive a date for a hearing to take place within one to three months of sending in the details of your appeal, depending on where you live.

The tribunal hearing will be relatively informal (compared with a court hearing), and the case will be adjudicated by a panel of experts, some lawyers and some not, and ultimately by the tribunal chairman. You may be represented before the tribunal or you may represent yourself. Ask your Citizens' Advice Bureau or Law Centre about having someone to represent you, since the Department of Social Security will certainly have employed a lawyer to put their argument. Unfortunately there is no legal aid available for tribunal representation.

If the decision of the tribunal also goes against you, your only remaining chance of appeal is to the Social Security Commissioner. The Commissioner can only hear appeals where it can be shown that the tribunal has made an error of law in reaching a decision in your case. Otherwise the decision of the tribunal is final.

Decisions made by benefit officers over grants from the social fund (see above) cannot be taken to the tribunal for appeal. The only way to appeal against a decision not to grant you a social fund payment is to ask for your case to be referred to the local social fund inspector.

2: The Right to an Education

Since the Education Act of 1944 it has been the right of every child and young person (at present up to the age of 16) to receive a full-time education in a State school. Some parents choose to send their children to privately funded, independent schools. Most of the information contained in this chapter relates to both State and private schooling. Where it does *not* apply in the case of private schooling, this will be made clear.

State education is controlled by a Government department, the Department of Education and Science (DES), and by local education authorities in each area of England and Wales. It is the officers of their education authority with whom most parents will deal, unless they make a special appeal (see below) to the DES.

A. CHOICE OF SCHOOLING

Does the State have any legal duty to provide schooling for the under-fives?
No. They have only a legal power (under the Education Act 1980) to establish schools for the under-fives if they so wish. This will depend on how important your education authority considers the question of under-fives' education to be, and what resources they have to spend in this area. If you feel that the local provision could be better, you should lobby your local councillor.

If your child is assessed as having 'special educational needs' (see below), then the authority does have a duty to provide appropriate educational facilities even under the age of five. This allows children with disabilities such as

17

deafness, or physical handicap, or mental handicap, or behavioural problems, any of which might affect their ability to learn, to receive special attention from an early age. It will probably be up to you as a parent to take the initiative and ask for an assessment of your child under five if you believe that he or she may have a 'special educational need' (see also below).

Is it true that it is parents who are responsible for ensuring that their children receive an education?
Yes. The Education Act 1944 places parents of children of school age (five to sixteen) under a legal obligation to ensure that they receive an appropriate education.

Parents may fulfil their responsibilities under the law by sending their children to a State school, a voluntary-aided school (see below) or a private school. In exceptional circumstances – such as where the child is ill, or the parents have other religious or moral grounds for not wishing to send the child to school – education may be provided at home (see below).

What if my child refuses to attend school?
Because the 1944 Education Act makes it the legal duty of every parent to ensure that their child receives a proper education, the law also makes parents responsible for their child's actual attendance at school. If your child is a persistent truant, the local education authority will contact you as the child's parent and remind you that it is your legal responsibility to ensure that your child attends school.

In some cases there may be very little you can do to persuade an older child to attend school if he or she is determined not to do so. The local authority (at present the Social Services Department; after the Children Act the Education Department) can place a child who is a non-school-attender under the supervision of a social worker or an education social worker by asking for a 'supervision' order from a magistrates' court. This means that the child will have to meet regularly with the supervisor who will try to improve his or her school attendance record.

In exceptional circumstances, the local authority may seek a full care order on a child who is beyond parental control and constantly truanting. Generally this will only occur where there are other problems in the family home of which the truanting is only a symptom (see Chapter 6).

Local authorities do have the power in law to prosecute parents whose children do not attend school. In practice this drastic step is usually only taken against a parent when they have refused to co-operate with the authority's officers and where one of the other approaches such as a supervision order has not worked or is not appropriate. Prosecutions usually only arise where the parent is using the child's non-school-attendance to make a personal protest (for example, against wearing school uniform, or the form of school assemblies, or sex education at school) rather than when the parent has obviously done his or her best to persuade the child to attend school.

Can I educate my child at home if I want to?

In exceptional circumstances – such as where the child is or has been ill, or where the parents have religious or philosophical grounds for not wishing their child to be educated in a school – education may be provided at home.

Generally speaking, if you wish to teach your child at home the education authority will be more concerned about the standard of the education that you can provide at home than your reasons for wishing to do so. You must still fulfil your duty under the 1944 Education Act (above) to ensure that your child receives a proper education, according to his or her needs and abilities. Therefore, if you are considering educating your child at home, you must appreciate that local education officers will need to be satisfied that your child is being properly educated and not being disadvantaged by your choice to educate him or her at home. They will want to see the curriculum of work planned for the child, the examinations (if appropriate) for which the child will be entered, and that the physical conditions of study at home are acceptable. They will also consider the suitability and qualifications of the individual – whether yourself or a tutor – who is to teach the child.

There are several schools near where we live. Can I choose which one I send my children to?
In the first instance, yes. The Education Act 1980 gives parents the right to state a preference for a particular school in their area. Moreover, the education authority must publish details of all the schools in its area to enable parents to make an informed choice.

The authority may refuse you your first choice of school if it can show that to admit your child to that particular school would be either an inefficient use of resources (for example, where your child would have to travel a long distance to attend that school) or where it would prejudice the efficient provision of education in that school for other children (for example, where your child has special learning needs which cannot be fulfilled given the facilities and staffing at that school without adversely affecting the provision made for the other children).

Under the Education Reform Act 1988, the authority is not allowed to refuse your child a place at a school where the number of children due to be admitted that year is less than the fixed 'standard number' for admission. Every school has a standard number for admissions and must continue to admit children until it reaches that figure (admissions to nursery education are excluded from this figure). Thus, even if your child does need to travel some distance to attend the school, this does not constitute a good reason for refusing a place where the school has not yet reached its target admissions number. This is known as 'open enrolment'.

The admission of children with learning difficulties to mainstream schools will be discussed in detail below.

In the case of schools which are 'voluntary-aided' (see below), the governing body may make a special arrangement with the local education authority to restrict admissions on criteria which maintain the 'special character' of the school. If you are considering sending your child to a voluntary-aided school you should find out if any such arrangement exists and if so what are its terms.

How would I appeal against the education authority's decision on my choice of school?

You may appeal first to the education authority itself. They must arrange for a formal hearing at which you can set out your grievance. The appeals panel will consist of up to seven people, some of whom will be officers of the authority and some will be independent members, for example local teachers, or councillors, or anyone with experience of education. You may wish to have someone to state your case at the hearing, perhaps a lawyer or a friend, who can set out your case objectively and persuasively.

Before the hearing, you must state, in writing, your reasons for making the appeal. At the hearing itself you may if you wish have a solicitor to represent you, but you may do just as well at this stage by putting your case yourself. You may want to ask someone with a relevant professional opinion on these matters (for example, your family doctor, social worker or a past teacher of your child) to come to the hearing and back up your case.

You must be notified in writing of the outcome of the local authority hearing. If you have been turned down and wish to take your appeal further, you may now appeal to the Secretary of State for Education and Science. A hearing will be arranged for you at the Department of Education and Science (DES) in London, where DES officials will listen to what you have to say. You may want a solicitor to speak for you at this stage but it is not essential if you feel confident you can manage without.

If the decision by the Secretary of State goes against you, the only remaining 'domestic' remedy open to you is to ask the High Court to conduct a 'judicial review' of the Minister's decision. This is an expensive process with only a small chance of success and you would need to consult with a solicitor with experience of judicial review. You may wish to consider other ways of putting pressure on the local authority, such as publicity, or making an application to the European Court of Human Rights in Strasbourg. You will have to talk to a solicitor or to a social action group (see Chapter 10, 'Getting Legal Advice and Representation') with experience in these matters if you wish to pursue this route.

One of our local schools is described as 'voluntary-aided'. What does this mean?

In a voluntary-aided school the local education authority and the school governors share the cost of running the school. The teaching staff are employed by the school governors and not by the local authority, which gives them a degree of autonomy in selecting staff beyond that of a State school, where the governors must agree new staff with the local authority.

Most voluntary-aided schools are run by church organizations who make up the funding after the local authority grant. If you are considering sending your child to a voluntary-aided school, you should consider whether your child will fit in with the particular religious or cultural orientation of the school and whether you as a parent are sympathetic to this approach.

You must also bear in mind that its voluntary-aided status means that the school will not be subject to local authority policies on, for example, racism, sexism and discipline, although they will of course be subject to any law prohibiting sexism, racism or corporal punishment. You may feel perfectly happy with the school's approach to these areas but you should find out in advance what position the school takes over these and other important issues.

What difference will it make if my child's school 'opts out' of local authority control?

Under the Education Reform Act 1988, every State school in England and Wales has the opportunity to conduct a ballot of parents on whether the school should break away from local authority control. If two-thirds of the total number of parents with children at the school (not two-thirds of those who actually vote) vote for opting-out, the school will gradually become independent from the local education authority and handle its own recruitment and contracts of employment, budgeting and maintenance. It will be known as a 'grant-maintained school'.

Most schools will need local authority help to become independent, both advice and cash assistance for the first few years. Many local authorities are making transitional arrangements with schools which have voted to opt out. These schools will eventually be financed not by the local authority but by the Secretary of State, that is, central rather than local government.

The governors of a grant-maintained school have more extensive powers than governors of schools staying within local authority control. Unlike governors at county or local authority controlled schools, they have the power to make decisions about spending and about the hiring and firing of school staff without the approval of the local authority (although governors of county schools will increasingly have autonomy in some areas as Local Management Schemes are implemented).* Since their responsibilities will be greater, much will depend, therefore, on your confidence in the schools' governors when you are considering the pros and cons of the school's opting-out.

The implications for your child's education of the school deciding to 'opt out' are therefore much the same as for a voluntary-aided school (see above). If you feel that the school governors will make a better job of running the school, recruiting the teachers, drawing up a school budget and maintaining the premises than the local authority has done, you should vote for opting out. Remember, though, that school governors can be in post for a maximum of four years and that the composition of the governing body may change during the time your child is at the school. Remember also that the new powers given to governors in grant-maintained schools are onerous and that most governors will have work commitments elsewhere. Finally, remember too that the decision to opt-out will inevitably result in a period of upheaval and uncertainty in the school, and that it can only be reversed by another ballot of parents.

---

*Some further examples of where governors of grant-maintained schools have more extensive powers than those of county schools are given later in this chapter.

B. OTHER CONSIDERATIONS AFFECTING SCHOOL CHOICE

I am anxious about my son taking part in sports such as rugby. What liability, if any, does the school have if he is injured?

Schools have only a very limited liability for any accidents leading to injuries to pupils during school hours. The school must be insured against any accident which could have been prevented by their taking reasonable care; for example, you would expect appropriate safety facilities to be available for chemistry lessons, for children to receive proper instruction before handling any potentially dangerous substances and, since a recent case, for sports lessons, to avoid school age children playing against adults (e.g. the 'old boys' side).

Playing sport is considered to be a normal part of school life which requires the school authorities only to take reasonable care with the provision of facilities, etc. The result is that if your son is injured while playing rugby, there is little chance that the school will be held liable to compensate for his injuries unless there has been negligence. You may wish to take out personal accident insurance on his behalf.

I object to my children taking part in a Christian or other form of religious assembly at school. What can I do about it?

The law demands that all schools provide an opportunity for pupils to take part in 'collective worship' on each school day, and that this collective worship should be of a 'broadly Christian nature'.

Both schools and individual pupils may be exempted from this requirement. Schools where the majority of pupils are from non-Christian backgrounds, for example, may apply for exemption from this requirement to an advisory council set up by the local authority.

Individual pupils may also be excused on the request of a parent from attending the act of collective worship. They may be similarly excused from religious instruction where it forms part of the curriculum (see below).

My child has special religious and dietary requirements which I want him to observe during the school day. Can I ask his school to make arrangements for this?

The Education Reform Act 1988 allows you to request that your child is withdrawn from school for the purpose of receiving religious instruction which is not available at the school he or she attends. Although you have the right to request that your child be excused from school in order to attend elsewhere (for example a mosque or synagogue) for religious instruction, the school may refuse if this interferes with his or her attendance at regular classes during the school day.

Since the provision of school meals is now a matter for the discretion of each education authority (see also below), the law says nothing about any right to ask for a special diet for your child. In practice, where the school provides meals for pupils, provision can be made on request to meet any special dietary requirements.

Is the education authority obliged to provide my child with free school meals or milk?

No. Since the Education Act 1980 there has been no legal duty for schools to provide free milk and/or meals except in the exercise of a discretion – such provision 'as seems requisite' by the authority. Whether any authority provides milk and meals to schools in its area will depend, therefore, on how they choose to exercise this discretion.

Is my child entitled to free medical and dental checks at school?

Yes. Under the National Health Service Act 1977 every local authority should provide facilities for medical and dental inspections of pupils at regular intervals. Where schools are no longer under local authority control (see 'opting-out' above), each grant-maintained school will decide whether to offer such facilities.

What obligations do schools have to prevent sex or race discrimination?

The same obligations as any other organization under the Sex Discrimination Act 1975 and the Race Relations Act 1976; that is to prevent any direct or indirect discrimination on the grounds of sex or racial origin. Direct discrimination prevents schools, for example, from exercising quotas for the number of girls or boys they will admit. Indirect discrimination means attaching conditions to the provision of a service (in this case education) which makes it available to less people of one sex or race than those of another sex or race. Under the law some restrictions, for example on the wearing of a certain form of dress, may be justified by considerations of safety. Where possible, schools can and do make arrangements to accommodate religious and cultural reasons for the wearing of certain forms of dress (for example when swimming or in PE lessons).

C. THE SCHOOL CURRICULUM

What will the 'National Curriculum' mean for my child's schooling?

The National Curriculum is being phased into all schools (primary and secondary) from September 1989. It requires schools to provide a 'core' of three taught subjects, mathematics, science, and English. In addition each secondary school is expected to instruct its pupils in history, geography, technology, music, art, one foreign language and physical education. Religious instruction remains a compulsory part of the curriculum for all pupils, subject to the exceptions discussed above.

In most schools little in the actual content of the curriculum will change as a result of the National Curriculum. What is more likely to affect the nature of your child's education is the parallel requirement that all children should be tested to nationally devised standards in subjects which they are studying at ages seven, eleven, fourteen and sixteen.

I don't like the way that sex education is taught at my child's school. What can I do about it?
As the law stands, you only have the right to withdraw your child from religious instruction (see above). In practice and in law the manner in which sex education is taught at a particular school is the responsibility of the governors. Therefore any complaints you have should be addressed to them.

I heard that under the new law schools are allowed to charge for some services. Is this right and what sort of things might I be charged for?
With effect from 1 April 1989, schools under local authority control have the right to charge parents for any activities which take place outside school hours (for example a residential field trip over a weekend, or a visit to a theatre in the evening). Where an activity takes place partly in and partly outside school time, the guiding principle is whether more than 50% of the time falls outside school hours. If it does, then a charge can be levied. It is for each authority to decide whether or not to pass this cost on to parents, how much should be charged

and a policy of remissions for those who have difficulty meeting the charge.

Schools can also charge parents for individual tuition, for example music lessons, where the instruction does not form part of the National Curriculum or the syllabus for an examination.

Equipment such as books, stationery and ingredients or materials for cooking or craft and design classes must be provided free by the school but parents may be asked to contribute to these costs on a voluntary basis and may actually be formally charged where they have asked for the finished product, for example an article made in a craft and design class or food prepared in a cookery lesson.

D. DISCIPLINE

Who has final authority in deciding what standards of discipline are to be applied in each school?

In a State school it is the governors who are responsible in law for the measures of discipline which are used in the school by the teachers. Some local education authorities recommend guidelines for punishments. In the first instance it is the governing body who will hear any complaints about standards of discipline and punishments, with a further appeal to the local education authority where the school is under LEA control. In practice, the head teacher of a school makes most of the important on-the-spot decisions about discipline which may affect your child. It is important, therefore, that in deciding upon a school for your child you meet and talk to the head teacher.

Are the teachers at my child's school entitled to use corporal punishment (e.g. cane, slap with a ruler)?

No. Since the Education Act 1986 no teacher at a State school (whether or not 'opted-out') has been permitted (physically) to punish a child in any way whatsoever. Any teacher who does so risks dismissal by his employer and court action by a parent.

If you want to find out more about the standards of discipline which operate at your child's school (or prospective school) you should read the school regulations carefully and ask the head teacher if you have any queries. Remember that even if the regulations state that discipline will be at the head teacher's discretion (which is a common form) this must not include any physical punishments, since these are now against the law.

My son has come home with a letter saying that he is suspended from attending school for one week because of bad behaviour. On what grounds is the school allowed to suspend him, and can we appeal?

The only restriction placed upon the school's decision to suspend a child (now called 'exclusion') is that it must be 'reasonable', i.e. it must be an appropriate response to his behaviour. In reality this gives the school, and specifically the head teacher, a very wide discretion in deciding upon the grounds for an exclusion.

You must be informed of your child's exclusion, and the reason for it, as soon as possible. If the exclusion is for more than five days in any one term, or will cause your child to miss an examination, the head teacher must also inform the governors and the local education authority without delay. This means that, if you do decide to appeal (below), the governors and the authority should already be apprised of the facts of the case if it is a five day or indefinite exclusion or will result in your child missing an examination.

You may appeal to the school governors against the decision to exclude your child. They may direct that your child is reinstated. If they uphold the school's decision, you may, if the school is under local authority control, appeal next to a specially constituted education authority appeal panel. If the school has 'opted-out' (see above), your only line of appeal after the governors is to the Secretary of State for Education.

My son's school has written to me to say that they are excluding him until he gets his hair cut and wears the correct school uniform. Can they exclude him from the school on these grounds and must we comply if he is to return to this school?
The school may exclude your son on any grounds which they consider to be 'reasonable' (see above). If conditions are set for re-entry, as in this case, they must relate to 'reasonable' standards of school discipline. Your son's school could argue (and in this they are supported by legal precedent) that neatly cut hair and wearing the school uniform are matters of school discipline.

The European Convention on Human Rights, to which the United Kingdom is a signatory, stipulates that parents cannot be forced to accept school rules which conflict with their own genuinely held views on education. This provision has ben used, for example, to force the UK Government to ban corporal punishment in schools. It appears to have only limited further application and has been held not to apply to, for example, parental objections to sex education. It is unlikely, therefore, that it could be used to support an argument that you are philosophically opposed to the wearing of school uniform. Although the education authority must make schooling available to your child, they could argue that they discharge this duty by providing other schools in the area which do not require the wearing of school uniform; or, if there are no local schools which do not have uniform requirements, that to provide a school which does not impose a uniform is an inefficient use of their resources. In either case, if your son does not comply with the school rules and return to school, you are liable for prosecution (see above) for failing to ensure that he is receiving an education.

I cannot afford to buy my child's school uniform. The school says that they won't accept him without the uniform. What can I do?

Most education authorities operate a grants system for parents who find buying the school uniform a real hardship.

My daughter's school has written to me saying that they intend to expel her for bad behaviour. On what grounds are they entitled to expel her?

As we have already seen to be the case with exclusions (see above), the head teacher has an ultimate discretion to exclude or expel pupils on 'reasonable' disciplinary grounds. Where a child is to be permanently excluded, i.e. expelled, the school must provide parents with a full 'statement of decision', giving the reasons for the expulsion. An appeal can be made in the same way as for exclusions (see above).

Where a pupil is expelled from a maintained school the local education authority is obliged to accommodate him at another school if he is under compulsory school age or if his parents wish it. Obviously this creates administrative and education problems and, in general, local authorities discourage expulsions for anything other than very serious reasons.

Am I entitled to access to my child's school record? Can I appeal against anything which is written there if I feel that it is unfair?

There is no law which gives you the right to see your child's school record. The only law which relates to this concerns the holding of information on computer disc. If your child's record is held on computer disc, the school must give you access to it if they hold it for more than 40 days i.e. if it is a permanent record.

The 1988 Education Act provides for the Secretary of State for Education to make regulations as to the persons who are entitled to see records of your child's achievement in the national curriculum tests administered at seven, eleven, fourteen and sixteen. These regulations have not yet appeared but they will probably give parents the right to see such records. This applies only to test results and not to other information which may be held on your child's file.

Obviously, without seeing the file you cannot appeal against anything written on it. If you are given access to your child's file and dispute something which appears there, you can complain as above, first to the governors and then to the education authority; unless the school has 'opted-out' in which case appeal should be made first to the governors and then to the Secretary of State. The only basis for an appeal is that the information you are challenging is 'unreasonable'.

E. SPECIAL EDUCATION

I think that my son may have learning difficulties and I would like him to be professionally assessed. What are the local education authority's duties?

Under the Education Act 1981, education authorities are given special legal responsibilities for children who appear to have learning difficulties. Learning difficulties are defined as:

(a) significantly greater difficulty in learning than the majority of children in the same age group; *or*

(b) a disability which prevents or hinders a child from using the educational facilities provided for children of his age in that area – for example, a physical disability.

If you or anyone else, such as the child's teachers or the family doctor or social worker, feel concerned about your child's development and ability to learn, you may ask the education authority to make a formal assessment of his 'special educational needs'. Once your child's difficulties have been brought to the attention of the education authority they are obliged in law to undertake an assessment (unless they can show that the request for an assessment is 'unreasonable'). Where the child is under the age of two, the authority cannot carry out the assessment without the parent's consent.

The Education Act 1981 also gives parents rights to be involved in the process of assessment itself. The parent may ask that a particular individual (for example, a doctor or psychologist who already knows the child) should be consulted in the assessment process. This right also allows parents to decide how many medical examinations are carried out on their child in the course of the process of 'statementing', whether they wish to be invited to attend 'case conferences' on their child's case involving

34

social workers, education officers and medical personnel, and so on.

At the end of the assessment process (which may take up to three months) the authority will send you a 'statement of special educational needs'. This is a written form which describes the results of the assessment process and any particular difficulties identified during the assessment which may affect your child's development and ability to learn. These may be medical, psychological or behavioural difficulties – the important thing is that they are preventing him from learning at the same pace as his peers.

The 'statement' will also make recommendations as to the form of education from which your child will, in the opinion of the authority, most benefit. It will recommend a place in a particular school.

You may wish to ask for further explanation of what the statement says, in which case the authority must assist you in clarifying its conclusions. If you want to challenge any of the conclusions of the statement, including the choice of recommended school, you may appeal first to the authority itself and then to the Secretary of State (as for 'discipline' and 'choice of school' above).

The education authority has written to me to say that they want to carry out an assessment of my son's 'special educational needs', but I feel that he is happy in his present school and that this would be disruptive and unnecessary. Can I object to the assessment being carried out?

If your son is under two, the authority cannot proceed without your consent (see above). If your son is over two, you may appeal first to the authority and ultimately to the Secretary of State against the decision to carry out an assessment. You must put your reasons in writing, and if possible obtain the written support of a relevant professional (your family doctor, social worker, your son's teachers) for your objection to the assessment being carried out.

I don't want my child to go to a 'special school' but to a mainstream school with special classes for 'slow learners'. Do I have the right to demand this?

Although the Education Act 1981 places education authorities under a duty to provide integrated schooling wherever possible for children of all learning abilities, in practice this duty can be compromised if the authority can show that to provide a place in a mainstream school for your child would:

(a) prevent your child receiving the special education he is believed to need; *or*

(b) conflict with the provision of 'efficient education' for the other children in that school – for example where there are insufficient resources or staff in that school to provide the necessary supervision for mixed ability groups; *or*

(c) prevent the efficient use of resources within the authority.

The result of this in practice is that authorities which do not have 'special needs units' within mainstream schools cannot, at present, be forced to admit your child to a mainstream school or to provide 'slow learner units' where none currently exist. Some authorities have taken steps to ensure that a large number of the children assessed as having 'special educational needs' within their area do have the chance to take up a place (at least part-time) in a special needs unit in a mainstream school. Others have very few or no places like this on offer. If you live within an authority which does not make such provision but maintains strictly segregated schooling for children with special needs, you should lobby your local councillors and the education officers to alert them to the demand for places for children with special needs in units which are part of mainstream schools. You could contact the CSIE (the Centre for Studies on Integration in Education) for further help and advice (see Chapter 10, 'Getting legal advice and representation').

Our local school is threatened with closure because of falling rolls. How can we fight this?

Firstly, education authorities have a duty to 'consult' with the local community over a proposed school closure. The precise meaning of this is unclear. It seems that it must include providing sufficient information about plans for alternative schooling for the pupils at present educated at the school. It must allow sufficient time for the community to consider the proposals and cope with their implementation.

When the authority publishes the notice of its intention to close your school, you have the right to submit your objections to the education authority within two months of the notice being made. An objection must come from a minimum of ten local government electors (i.e. ten people on the local government electoral register) or from individuals where they are governors of a school with 'voluntary-aided' status (see above). The authority must send your objections on to the Secretary of State who will take the final decision over closure.

The grounds on which the Secretary of State will take this final decision are also imprecise. He must consider the educational and financial advantages of closing the school, but must also place these considerations within the context of the preferences of the local community and, in particular, parents. If the Secretary of State's decision goes against you, the only legal option left open to you is to ask the High Court to review the decision. This is a very costly process and has only a slim chance of success unless you can show that the decision is clearly 'unreasonable'. Nonetheless some parents have success-fully fought school closures using this route. Often the best that an application to the High Court for review will do is to delay the eventual closure by a few more months, and in some cases this may make it a tactic worthy of consideration.

3: Children and the Criminal Justice System

At what age does a child become liable to prosecution under the criminal law?
Children may be charged with a criminal offence from the age of ten. The law considers that by this age it is possible to establish a criminal 'intent', that is a deliberate decision to do something which is antisocial and against the law.

Up to what age is a young person classified as a 'juvenile offender'?
Up to and including 17 years of age. The application of the law – for example the maximum period of detention permitted – does vary according to both age and sex (see below).

Are parents ever liable on behalf of their children for the crimes they commit?
In some circumstances parents may be liable to pay the fines incurred by their children and they may be 'bound over' to keep their son or daughter out of trouble in future (see below).

Are there any special defences open to children?
No. For anyone, child or adult, to be convicted of a crime the prosecuting authorities (the State, represented by the police and the Crown Prosecution Service) must usually show deliberate intent. This may be more difficult to prove with a very young offender.

A. YOUNG PEOPLE AND THE POLICE

Can the police insist on carrying out a search in the street on a child or a young person?

Yes. A police constable, in or out of uniform, has the legal power to stop anyone of any age whom he suspects of either carrying an offensive weapon or stolen goods, and 'frisk' search them in the street. If you are stopped in the street there are several points to remember about how the police are permitted to exercise this power:

(a) the police officer must tell you his name and the station to which he is attached, and give you the reason for the search. If he is out of uniform, he must show you some evidence that he is a police officer. If you are stopped and searched by the police without this information being given, you should make a point of asking for it. If the information is refused you are, strictly speaking, being unlawfully searched;

(b) if you are stopped in a public place, you can only be asked to remove your overcoat, or empty your pockets. If the police wish to carry out a search involving the removal of any other clothing, you must be taken to a 'private place', for example the back of a police van. The police may use only 'reasonable force' in carrying out this search;

(c) if there is nowhere private nearby to carry out a more extensive search, the police may want to take you back to the station for this purpose. If you are not willing to go voluntarily, then you can only be forced to go if you are arrested and formally detained. This means that you must be 'cautioned' (see below) and given a reason for your arrest.

Do I have to give the police my name and address if they stop me in the street and ask me who I am?

You would be well advised to do so, since the police may arrest you if you withhold your name and address or if you give a name and address which they suspect to be false. The justification for this is that without your (accurate) name and address they would be unable to go to a magistrate to get a warrant to arrest you at a later date. Even if this doesn't seem like a very good justification to you, it would be better to co-operate with such a request.

Can the police take away anything they find if they stop and search me in the street?

If something is discovered during the course of the search which gives rise to a criminal charge – for example, illegal drugs, stolen goods or an offensive weapon – then this will be seized by the police and you can be arrested and taken to the local station to be charged (see below for your rights at the police station).

Sometimes the police may decide to confiscate the illegal or stolen goods – for example a small amount of cannabis – and let you go on your way without arresting and charging you. Although strictly speaking you should be arrested and charged if your property is confiscated because it is illegal or has been stolen, this is not something you would generally argue about – unless, of course, the property confiscated was not illegal or stolen at all.

Can I be questioned by the police at school?

Yes, but only in the presence of the head teacher or another teacher.

Can the police ask a juvenile to go to the police station to be questioned?

The police may ask anyone of any age to go to the police station to 'assist them with their inquiries'. The decision to go or not is purely voluntary. If you don't want to go, the only way you can be lawfully made to is by arresting you (see below).

What is the difference between 'assisting with inquiries' and being arrested?

If you are arrested, the police have the legal power to detain you against your will, usually in a police station. You should also be informed of the fact and the grounds of your arrest and given a formal 'caution', explaining that 'you do not have to say anything unless you wish to, but anything you say may be used in evidence'.

If you are merely 'assisting with inquiries', and are not subsequently placed under arrest, you are free to leave the police station at any time you want. You too will be given a formal 'caution' before you are questioned, but this does not mean that you are under arrest.

When I start being questioned, do I have to answer questions if I don't want to or think it is better if I don't?

You may refuse to answer any questions and your silence cannot be interpreted by a court at a later stage as a suggestion that you are guilty (although there are proposals to change the law).

Whether or not you are prepared to answer questions, you should always wait until you have contacted an adult (for example, your parent, friend, social worker or solicitor) who will sit in on the interview. The police are not supposed to begin to question a juvenile until such a person has arrived unless they can show that any delay will result in *serious* risk to persons or property (for example if it is suspected that a robbery or an assault is about to be carried out which you have information about), and you should insist that no interview begins without an adult being present.

Do I have the right to phone my parents, friend, social worker or a solicitor?

Yes. In the case of juveniles, the police themselves are obliged under their Code of Practice to inform an adult of your detention (your parents if you live at home, your social worker and also your supervisor if you are under a supervision order; see below). They must explain the reasons for your arrest to this adult once he or she arrives.

In addition, you have a right like any other detained person to contact someone outside (for example a friend) and to request legal advice. It is up to you to exercise these rights and make these requests, although the custody officer at the police station is supposed to tell you that you have these rights and sometimes there may be notices displayed to this effect.

The only circumstances under which you may be refused a telephone call to a named person or to a solicitor is firstly where the superintendent at the station decides that any contact with the person you have asked to call could interfere with the investigation of the case (for example, it could lead to a 'tip-off' to someone else involved or the disposal of stolen goods). Second, you must have been arrested for a 'serious offence' which would include firearms offences, sexual offences such as rape or sexual assault, obviously murder or manslaughter, or any offence involving large amounts of money or property, or serious injury to anyone. Even if you are refused a telephone call on these grounds, this can only be for a maximum of 36 hours and you would be well-advised to wait until an adult is present before answering questions.

What happens if I don't know any solicitors, and neither do my parents?

Every police station in England and Wales now operates a 'duty solicitor' scheme which means that there is a rota of local solicitors available to come to the station at any time to act as a legal adviser to someone who has been arrested and detained. There may be notices in the station to this effect giving details and phone numbers, or you may have to ask the custody officer for this information.

Will I have to pay the solicitor?

Not at this stage. If your case comes to trial you may be awarded criminal legal aid if you or your parents are assessed as having insufficient means to pay for legal representation (see below).

Can the police keep me in the police station overnight?

Yes, but, as a juvenile, you may not normally be kept in a cell. The Code of Practice says that you can only be locked up in a cell if your behaviour is such that there is genuine alarm that you may injure yourself or others or property unless you are restrained. You may also be locked up in a cell if there is no one available to otherwise supervise you. If you are placed in a cell, there must be a written record of the reasons for this.

You may never be placed in a locked cell with a detained adult.

For how long can I be questioned without a break?

The Code of Practice says that you must have eight consecutive hours free from questioning in any 24 so that you can rest. You should also have breaks for meals and refreshment. If during your questioning you feel that you have not had a break for a long time or you want something to eat or drink and this request is refused, you should ask to have this fact recorded in the interview record. The adult who will be with you (your parent, friend, social worker, solicitor or any other adult) should be aware also that any complaint by them about your treatment must be entered in the interview record.

Can the police insist on taking a child's fingerprints?

Generally speaking, fingerprinting may only take place with consent which, for a child under 16, will probably be taken to mean the consent of his or her parents. Fingerprinting may take place without consent where the superintendent of the police station authorizes this on the grounds that the fingerprinting will confirm or otherwise that the detainee has commited an offence. Therefore, forcible fingerprinting can only take place where the child is old enough to be charged with an offence i.e. ten years of age.

Can the police insist on carrying out a body search at a police station on a child or young person?

Once again, only on the authorization of the station superintendent and only where either:

(a) it is suspected that the child has concealed a weapon in his body orifices with which he may injure himself or others; *or*

(b) he is suspected of hiding Class A drugs (heroin, cocaine) in his body orifices.

The search may only take place in the presence of the accompanying adult (see above) and if not carried out by a doctor must be conducted by a police officer of the same sex as the person being searched.

What happens if I am held and questioned in the police station for eight hours and then released without charge?

The law allows the police to arrest you and detain you in a police station where you will be questioned for up to 24 hours. After 24 hours the police must decide either to charge you with an offence (which means that you will be scheduled to appear in the juvenile court; see below), or release you without bringing any charges.

You may be detained without charge for a further 12 hours (i.e. a total of 36 hours), but only if the station superintendent believes that a further period of questioning before you are formally charged is necessary to secure or safeguard evidence *and* that you have committed a 'serious arrestable offence' (see above).

After 36 hours, you must either be charged or released without charge, or in exceptional circumstances the police may apply to two magistrates to detain you for a further 36 hours without charge. Different provisions cover the detention of suspected terrorists.

After being arrested and questioned, the police have sent me home on 'police bail' and say that I must report back in two weeks' time. What does this mean will happen to me? Will I have to go to court?

Possibly not. The police have the right to place you on police bail once you have been formally arrested, with a requirement that you report back at a given time after they have made more inquiries. It does not depend on you being charged (see below).

Once you are released on police bail, the file on your case will probably be sent to the juvenile bureau for consideration. The juvenile bureau is staffed by police officers and social workers. They may decide to caution you, which means that when you return to the police station you will be formally reprimanded and this will appear on your police record. They may decide to charge you with an offence, or they may decide to do nothing at all and when you return to the police station you will be told that the case has been dropped.

I have been charged by the police after questioning and sent home. What happens next?

You will be scheduled to appear in the juvenile court to answer the charge or charges against you. If you haven't consulted a solicitor up to now, you should arrange an appointment with a local legal aid solicitor and take along your charge sheet. You should also ask one or both of your parents, or whoever is responsible for you, to go along with you since they will need to sign the means form for legal aid assessment if you are under 16.

Are the police allowed to stop me going home after I have been charged?

You may only be detained after you have been charged if one of the following grounds is made out in your case:

(a) there is doubt as to the authenticity of your name and address;

(b) there is a genuine fear that you might interfere with witnesses, or commit further offences;

(c) there is a genuine belief that you will not answer bail (see also below);

(d) it is necessary to keep you in police custody for your own safety.

If the police believe that one of these grounds exists in your case, you must appear before the juvenile court as soon as possible, usually the same day or the day after you have been charged, for a bail hearing. If the court decides not to release you or to bail you on conditions (see below), you will normally be placed in the care of the local authority, that is, a residential home or sometimes secure accommodation provided by the local authority (see Chapter 5 under 'emergencies') until the date of the full hearing of your case in the juvenile court (see below).

On what grounds is bail awarded and what conditions might be attached?

If the police oppose bail and believe that you should be kept in custody, they must show to the satisfaction of the juvenile court panel, that you are either:

  (a) likely to abscond before the hearing of your case;
  (b) likely to commit another offence in the meantime;
  (c) likely to 'obstruct the course of justice' by, for example, interfering with witnesses or warning off someone else involved in the crime with you.

If one or more of these grounds can be made out in your case, then you will be remanded into the care of the local authority (occasionally to a remand centre or prison; see below) until your trial.

Alternatively you may be granted bail but with conditions attached; for example, your parents may be asked to put up a surety to ensure your attendance at the trial, or you may be required to report regularly to a probation officer or the police station. Alternatively, the panel may be satisfied that no conditions are necessary in which case you will be able to go home until the date set for your trial.

Under what circumstances can a juvenile be remanded to a remand centre or prison?

The court may only order remand to a remand centre or prison if grounds are found for issuing an 'unruly certificate', which means that the juvenile is considered to be too unruly a character to be safely remanded into the care of the local authority. The court may only issue an unruly certificate where the charge is one which involves serious violence, and/or would carry a possible sentence of 14 years or more for an adult (known as a 'section 53' offence), and where the court is satisfied that, if placed in local authority accommodation, this young person would be a risk to himself and to others. Certificates are also issued where the young person charged has a history of absconding from local authority care or of being 'disruptive' whilst in local authority care.

B. YOUNG PEOPLE AND THE CRIMINAL COURTS

Which court hears the criminal charges brought against a juvenile?

The juvenile court hears all charges brought against a juvenile with the exception of homicide.

Who sits in the juvenile court?

The juvenile court is staffed by local magistrates who are members of the juvenile court panel for the area. Magistrates are not necessarily people with legal qualifications and members of the juvenile court panel tend to be people who have some experience of working with young people. Three magistrates sit at any one time and one acts as chair.

Is the juvenile court hearing open to the public?

No. Cases heard in the juvenile court are held 'in camera', which means that the general public are not allowed to sit in the public gallery as they are in the magistrates' court. Furthermore, the press are barred from attending unless the bench makes a special order allowing the case to be reported. Even if the case is reported, your name will not be given in any reports.

The court will expect one or both of your parents, or whoever has responsibility for you, to be there with you and will probably ask why they are not present if they do not come to court. If you want someone else in particular to be in court with you as moral support, the bench will normally allow this, but you should inform your solicitor in advance and he or she will ask on your behalf.

Can I have my own solicitor?
Yes. If you have been arrested and taken to a police station (see above), you may have been allocated a solicitor from the duty solicitor rota. If you want a different solicitor, possibly someone who is recommended to you, to represent you at the hearing, you should say so as soon as possible. It is important that whoever represents you has an opportunity to talk to you before your court appearance and decide how best to put your case.

How will I pay for the solicitor?
You will be entitled to criminal legal aid to cover the cost of your legal advice and representation if you or your parents cannot afford to pay for legal representation. If you are under 16 you can be assessed on your own means which should, in most cases, ensure that you are awarded legal aid.

What role does the juvenile court welfare officer play?
The welfare officer is employed by the court to make inquiries where appropriate into the background of a juvenile brought before the bench, and sometimes to prepare a report for the court (the 'social inquiry report'). The welfare officer will be concerned with finding out about the young person's family background, how he or she is regarded by schoolteachers, any social workers involved with the family and where relevant any record of employment.

Where the welfare officer makes a written report, this must be shown to all parties, including the juvenile, before the court hearing (see also below).

What is the 'social inquiry report'?

Before a hearing in the juvenile court, a social inquiry report on the young person, giving the court information about his or her background, family, and anything else which may be relevant to the charge, is prepared by the court welfare officer (see above), a probation officer or a social worker and distributed to all the parties. There is a recommendation that this should take place at least 7 days before the hearing. The court may make a special order that there should be no report, but this only happens when, for example, a report has been put together on the same young person within the very recent past and there is nothing more to add.

Will I have the chance to see the social inquiry report myself?

You have the right to see the social inquiry report and may want to discuss with your solicitor how you should respond to what it says about you. Under exceptional circumstances, the court may make an order preventing you from seeing some or all of the report if it contains information which is considered to be harmful to you, for example, details of your parents' marital problems. You cannot be prevented from seeing any details which relate to the report writer's assessment of your own character.

Will I have to answer questions in court?

You do have the right to remain silent, like an adult charged with a criminal offence, although the court is permitted to draw its own (usually adverse) conclusions from your silence. In your own interests, unless you have reasons (which you should discuss with your solicitor) you should go to court prepared to answer the questions put to you by your own legal representative and by the prosecution lawyer.

Your solicitor should prepare you in advance for the

questions he or she will ask you and give you an idea of what you may be asked in addition by the prosecution (acting for the State) and the magistrates on the Bench. You should think about how you would answer questions and try to be well prepared and calm by the time you go to court.

Obviously you may be asked something you are not prepared for, or something which you feel is unfair or difficult to answer. Try to keep calm and answer questions as clearly as you can. It is not just what you say but how you say it which will influence the Bench when they come to decide whether or not you are guilty of the offence and, in particular, if they do find you guilty, what sort of sentence is appropriate. For the same reason, you should try to go to court neatly dressed and treat the proceedings seriously.

Can I appeal if I am found guilty?
Yes, you may appeal to the Crown Court.

C. CUSTODIAL SENTENCES

Does the juvenile court have the power to give me a custodial sentence?
Yes, but only where one or more of the following conditions are fulfilled:

(a) there is a history of failure to respond to non-custodial sentences in your case; that is, you have re-offended;

(b) only a custodial sentence would protect the public from harm from you;

(c) your offence was so serious that a non-custodial sentence cannot be justified.

The same principle applies to all those convicted of a crime up to the age of 21. In addition, where a crime has been committed by anyone under 21 which would be punishable with imprisonment if it were committed by an adult of 21 or older, then a custodial sentence must be passed on them.

If the panel does decide to pass a custodial sentence, they must give one or more of the above as reason(s) for the decision and explain this reasoning to you.

How long can I be sentenced to serve?
This depends on your age and sex.

A boy under 15 years old, or a girl under 17, can be sentenced to a maximum of four months in custody. If you are sentenced to two or more terms of custody to run consecutively, then the total term (the sum of each of the custodial terms you receive) must not exceed four months.

A boy aged 15 or 16 can be sentenced to a maximum of 12 months in custody.

At 17 or older either a young woman or a young man may be sentenced to life imprisonment.

Can a juvenile be sentenced to serve time in an adult prison or a remand centre?
Only on the direction of the Secretary of State, and then for a temporary period only.

What does it mean if a court sentences a young person to be 'detained at Her Majesty's pleasure'?
If a juvenile is convicted of what is known as a 'section 53' offence (defined as a crime which can attract a prison sentence of 14 years or more for an adult; for example, murder, manslaughter, rape, robbery and grievous bodily harm with intent), the court may order that he or she is 'detained at Her Majesty's pleasure', i.e. indefinitely or until it appears safe to release him or her.

D. NON-CUSTODIAL SENTENCES

1. Attendance Centre Orders

These are orders requiring your attendance at a centre (sometimes an 'intermediate treatment' centre) at the weekends for a specified period.

2. Probation/Supervision Orders

These may last for up to three years. If you are under 13 your probation will be supervised and monitored by a social worker; at 13 or over you will be assigned a probation officer.

I have been put on probation for a year. What does this mean?

You will be assigned a probation officer (see above) to whom you will be expected to report on a regular basis. The terms of your probation order will stipulate how often you should meet and where. The probation officer will keep a record of these meetings and any other information (for example, any occasion during your period of probation when you are in trouble with the police) which may be considered relevant to a review of your case at the end of your period of probation.

Your probation officer may be empowered under the probation order to require you to take part in such 'intermediate treatment' activities as are available in your area. These might include participation under supervision at a day training centre, or a boys' or girls' club.

The terms of your probation may also include restrictions on where you may spend the night and on particular activities, for example, visiting particular individuals or going to football matches. Your parent or guardian will have to agree to these and any other terms included in the order.

Can I choose who I have as my probation officer?
No. Generally the person assigned to your case will be someone who has some knowledge of you and it makes sense if this is someone you can get along with. If you feel particularly unhappy with the officer assigned to you, all you can do is ask, clearly stating your reasons, for someone else to be assigned to your case.

What happens if I break the terms of my probation?
You will have to return to the juvenile court and you will probably be fined. Depending on how you broke your terms, your period of probation could be further extended. The juvenile court also has the power to order a custodial sentence, probably for less than three weeks, if they feel that this is a necessary deterrent (see above).

3. Fines

If I am fined by the court, will I have to pay it all at once?
No. You can agree payment by instalments with the court clerk.

What happens if I don't pay?
If you fail to pay, the court clerk will attempt to enforce the fine, for example by writing to you or bringing you back to the court. Failure to pay on time may result in a second fine. If you are under 17, you cannot be sent to prison for failing to pay a fine and instead your parents may be made to pay the fine on your behalf.

4. Community Service Orders

Community service orders are an alternative to a custodial sentence for offenders aged 16 and over. They are made only where the same crime, if committed by an adult, would have been punishable with a prison term. Community service orders stipulate a number of hours in total which must be worked (between 40 and 120 for 16 and 17 year olds) within the next 12 months. If you are placed on community service you will also be assigned a probation officer.

What sort of work does community service involve?

The court may only make a community service order if it is satisfied that there are local arrangements for community service which can accommodate you. Most local authorities have community service units which organize work in old people's homes, gardening, painting and decorating in other residential homes.

Do I have to do community service if I don't want to?

You must give your consent in court for the order to be made in the first place.

What happens if I don't carry out the work programme I have been assigned?

You will be brought back to the court and will almost certainly receive a custodial sentence.

5. Binding Over to Keep the Peace

The court may accept a 'recognizance' from the parents of the juvenile as an alternative to all the above. This means that the parent of the young person must place a surety with the court of a specified amount and take responsibility for the behaviour of their son or daughter for a specified period of time. If the terms of the binding over are broken within this time, the surety will be forfeit and the young person will have to return to court.

4: Parental Custody and Access to Children

The right of a parent, whether the father or the mother of a child, to live with the child, or to have access to him or her, is not an absolute right in law.

A hundred years ago, children were regarded as the property of their parents, both morally and economically. Since then, laws have been introduced which limit parental rights over their children to what is in the child's 'best interests'. For example, as we shall see in Chapters 5 to 7, the law now allows the State to intervene in families where parents cannot care or have not cared properly for their children. Similarly, where two parents are in dispute over which one of them the child should live with, neither can assert an absolute right to the child. Instead, the courts will decide with whom it is in the child's best interests to live.

The position is different in relation to children who have been born outside marriage. Whereas the parents of children born inside marriage share parental rights, in the case of children born to partners who are not married to each other it is the mother alone who is recognized as the legal 'parent' of the child. The natural father of a child born outside marriage has no legal rights without first proving that he is the father of the child; only then does he have the right in law to apply for custody or access. Therefore, in what follows below the word 'parent' is used to describe either both parents where they are married to one another, or the mother only where the child has been born outside marriage. The position of the natural father in the case of unmarried parents is discussed later in the chapter.

What is the meaning of 'custody'?

When a court orders that a person (usually a parent but sometimes a grandparent or other third party, such as an aunt, or a cousin, or a family friend) should have 'custody' of a child, the precise meaning of the order will vary from court to court. Different interpretations of what may be included within the legal rights of a person with custody has led to confusion and uncertainty. For this reason and others the new law will abolish the concept of 'custody' (see below).

Generally speaking, the person with custody of a child has the right in law to take all major decisions concerning the child's upbringing, for example where he lives, where he goes to school, when and where he goes on holiday, and so on.

What principles do the courts apply in resolving disputes over who should have custody?

The first and most important principle is the child's best interests, or welfare. In considering with whom the child should live and whom he should have contact with, the courts must place this consideration before the parent's genuine wish to live with or have regular contact with his or her child. In other words, the right of the child to security and happiness, both long- and short-term, takes precedence over any right of the parent to live with or see his or her child.

The 'welfare principle' as it is known is the 'umbrella' term for a range of factors the court should take into account in resolving a dispute over custody or access. These will include, for example, considering the wishes and feelings of the child (although the age and maturity of the child is relevant here), the effect of change in his or her circumstances (for example, moving from the home of one parent to live with the other), whether each parent can provide what is necessary materially for the child (for example, a home, food, clothes and so on, but not luxuries), the age and sex of the child (for example, statistics show that the courts are sometimes reluctant to award sole custody to the father where the child is very young and especially where a little girl is concerned.

What is meant by 'care and control'? Is it the same as 'custody'?

No. Under the present law it is not necessary for the person awarded custody to be the person with whom the child lives, although this is generally the case where custody is given to one person only. It is usually the case that where custody is awarded jointly to both parents (see below), the child will have his or her main home with one or the other of them, and this person will be said to have 'care and control'. The court will always make an order about who shall have 'care and control' (that is day-to-day charge of the child) at the same time as it makes an order for custody.

What are 'joint custody' orders?

The court may award custody to both parents jointly in which case they will continue to share the right to take major decisions about the child's upbringing. Usually the child will have his main home with one parent only and this person is awarded care and control (above).

Joint custody orders are made where the court feels that it is both possible and beneficial for the parents to continue to negotiate with one another and both to play an active role in their child's life. However, uncertainty over the extent of the rights (to take decisions, to be consulted) of the non-custodial parent has led to criticism of joint custody orders. Furthermore it is almost inevitable that the parent with 'care and control' will feel that, since any major decision is likely to affect their day-to-day life and the organization of their home, they should have 'first say'.

On the other hand, a 'non-custodial parent' can play only a minor role in the child's life and often contact is eventually lost altogether. It is this particular aspect of the operation of the present law on custody that has led to the changes made in the Children Act 1989 to encourage parents who have separated to continue to share responsibility for the upbringing of their child (see below).

What changes will the new law in the Children Act make?

When the relevant provisions of the Children Act come into force, the concept of custody will disappear. Instead, both parents (where they are married to one another) will continue to have what the new law describes as 'parental responsibility' for their child, regardless of where the child lives or how often either parent has contact with the child. So any decision which needs to be made about the child must in theory be taken by both parents together in the same way as would be expected if the parents were still married and living together.

Under the new law, instead of making orders for custody the courts will make orders concerning only the physical details of the child's life, that is, where he lives and how much contact he has with either parent. These will be known as 'residence' orders, and 'contact' orders. Both orders may be made in favour of more than one person.

Neither of these orders will affect the 'parental responsibility' which the natural parents retain in relation to a child (see above). If the child is fostered by another family, or a residence order is made in respect of a person who is not the child's natural parent, that person will have 'parental responsibility' for the duration of the order, along with the natural parents who will retain their legal 'parental responsibilities'.

The Children Act anticipates the same tensions over the sharing of rights between parents (or with a third party such as a foster parent) as are often experienced with 'joint custody' under the present system. The Children Act allows for the court to make two further orders to avert future disputes. These will be known as 'prohibited steps' and 'specific issue' orders.

In what circumstances is it anticipated that 'specific issue' and 'prohibited steps' orders will be made?

It is expected that these orders will be made where the court recognizes the possibility of a dispute between the parents at some time in the future on a specific matter. It may have become apparent during the course of the court case that, for example, the two parents disagree violently over what sort of schooling their child should receive. In this case, the court could make a 'prohibited steps' order obliging the parties to return to the court before either takes or puts into effect a decision on the child's schooling. The court would then act as an arbitrator in the dispute. Alternatively, the court may feel that the best course for the child is already clear and they could then make a 'specific issue' order ruling on the question of the child's education.

Apart from education, other areas which have been suggested as areas of possible intervention by the courts to avert future long-running disputes are: the child's religious upbringing, annual holiday arrangements, whether the parent with whom the child lives can move abroad with the child, for example to take up a new job, what surname the child should use, and so on. Often the practical value of these orders diminishes as the child gets older and has the right in an increasing number of areas (for example, obtaining contraception; see Chapter 10) to make his or her own decisions rather than have them taken by the parents.

Neither a 'prohibited steps' nor a 'specific issue' order shall be used where the same effect could be achieved by a residence or contact order.

I am prepared for my ex-wife to stay in our family home and for the children to live with her there. However, I am paying maintenance and I feel that I should still have a say in how the children are brought up. Does paying maintenance give me this right?

No. The payment of maintenance, whether by court order or not, is a separate matter in law from the question of custody, access and any other role in decision-making vis-a-vis your children (see also below).

Your right to be consulted on how your children are brought up will under the present law depend upon the order the court makes regarding custody. If your wife is sole custodian, most judges would consider that this gives her the right to take major decisions about the childrens' education, holidays, and any other aspect of their growing up. There is some controversy about how far you retain the right to be consulted (see above) and you should ask your solicitor about this.

If custody is shared, with 'care and control' to your wife, then your right to intervene will depend upon the sort of issues which arise. You will have the joint right with your wife to make major decisions about the children's upbringing, and any dispute between you will be resolved by the court (according to the welfare principle, see above). Your wife is entitled to make decisions about day-to-day matters since she is the party with physical 'care and control'.

What can I do to ensure that I continue to have a say in how my children grow up?

You could ask the court to make a joint custody order (see above). Alternatively, if your application is considered under the Children Act once the new law has come into effect, you may ask for a 'residence' order (see above) to be made in favour of both you and your wife. Even if your wife alone is granted a 'residence' order under the new law you will in any case retain equal 'parental responsibilities' with your wife. It is thought that this will mean that you will continue to share major decisions about the children as if you were still married and living together, although the court may rule on 'specific issues' (for example how and where your children are educated) or 'prohibited steps' (that is, decisions which may only be made after consulting the court) (see above).

I am prepared for my ex-wife to have custody of our three children but I still want to be able to see them on a regular basis. What steps should I take to ensure this?

You should apply for an order establishing your right to access to your children. You may apply either to the magistrates' court or to the county court.

The order will be made if the court is satisfied that it is in the best interests of the children for you to have access to them, and them to you. Access is regarded first and foremost as the right of the child, rather than the right of the parent. It is not necessary for you to show that your wife has restricted your access, or that you believe that she may do so in the future. The order will be granted to establish a legal framework for your continued contact with your children.

The order, if made, will probably be for 'reasonable access' for you and your wife to work out together. In the event of any dispute, you may return to the court and ask the judge to arbitrate. Sometimes, if you request this, an order for access will specify times and dates for access although the courts generally prefer to leave the possibility of some flexibility in the arrangements.

Under the new law in the Children Act 1989, the court will make 'contact' orders to replace access orders. As now, it may specify periods of access or leave this to the parents to arrange.

I am worried that my ex-husband will insist on our son going to his old school. I would much rather he attended the local school with his friends. Can I insist on this?

If you have sole custody of your son, you have a good chance of being able to take the decision over where he is educated (provided that it can be shown to be in his 'best interests'). Some judges feel that, even where the father has no custody rights, he still has the right to be consulted over decisions of this kind. So you should consider the practical arguments you would use to justify your choice of another school and in particular how these affect your day-to-day care and control of your son.

If you share custody, then you are obliged to reach any major decisions such as this one together with your ex-husband. If you cannot agree, the court will act as arbitrator. Your status as the person with care and control will be significant since you must carry the day-to-day responsibility of bringing up the child; for example, you will be the person who will have to take the child to school and collect him, or make arrangements for someone else to do so.

My child was born as a result of my relationship with my co-habitee, but that relationship is now over. What is my position on custody of my child?

As the mother of a child born outside marriage, you are

recognized in law as the sole parent. This means that you automatically have sole right to have your child to live with you, although you can claim maintenance for the child from your ex-boyfriend in the same way as any married woman can claim maintenance for her children from her husband or ex-husband (see below).

Your ex-boyfriend has had the right, since 1 April 1989, to apply under the Family Law Reform Act (which has now become part of the Children Act) for a joint parental responsibilities order which would give him equal rights with you. These orders are expected only to be made with the consent of both parties and usually where they are living together as man and wife (see below). He may also apply for custody and access to the child under the Guardianship of Minors Act (now amended by the Family Law Reform Act) or 'residence' and 'contact' orders once the Children Act is fully in force. In either case, the courts are unlikely to diminish your original position as the parent with sole rights and responsibilities (above) unless you are in agreement with any change or unless extreme circumstances suggest that you are unfit to take care of your child.

Does it make any difference that my boyfriend's name is on the child's birth certificate?

No. The fact that your ex-boyfriend's name appears as 'father' on your child's birth certificate does not make any difference to your sole rights as parent. If he chooses to seek an order for custody or access to be transferred to him, he can rely on the birth certificate as presumptive (but not conclusive) proof that he is the father of your child. In any case he will still have to show that it is in the child's best interests for the court to award him custody or access (see below).

I am the father of my ex-girlfriend's child and want to see my child regularly and maybe have him come to stay with me when he is older. My ex-girlfriend will not co-operate with this. What can I do to ensure that I can have access?

You have the right to apply for access to your child under the Guardianship of Minors Act, now amended by the Family Law Reform Act 1987. Under the new law in the Children Act access becomes known as 'contact'. If your paternity is disputed, you will have to prove to the satis-faction of the court that you are the child's biological parent. This can now be done conclusively using genetic finger-printing. If your name appears as 'father' on the child's birth certificate this will support your case but is not conclusive in itself.

Assuming that you are accepted as, or can prove, that you are the child's biological parent, the court must decide if it is in the child's best interests for you to have regular access. They must weigh in the balance the benefits both you but most importantly your child could receive from establishing and maintaining a relationship, along with any reasoned objections on the mother's side, and the effect upon the child's life of spending time in two homes with two separate parents. If you have been paying or intend to pay maintenance in respect of the child this does not give you the right to access but will strengthen your case since it shows that you are prepared to take some responsibility for the costs of bringing up your child.

If the court agrees to give you access, they may simply make an order for 'reasonable access', with the terms to be worked out between yourself and your ex-girlfriend. Alternatively, the court may stipulate how often and what type of access (i.e. 'staying' access of 'visiting' access) should take place, to avoid future disputes. So long as you keep to the terms of this agreement, the courts will usually be prepared to enforce an access order if your ex-partner does not co-operate. It is also possible that the court may feel that the resulting disruption to the child outweighs the benefits to him of seeing you on a regular basis.

My ex-girlfriend had our baby a year ago and is living alone with him in a hostel. I don't believe that she can care for him properly and I want to take over his upbringing myself. What rights do I have?

Under the Guardianship of Minors Act (above), now amended by the Family Law Reform Act 1987, you may apply to be given sole custody of your child. Once again, you will have to prove paternity if this is in dispute. The court will consider whether it is in the child's best interests to give you sole custody, and this will involve you showing that his mother is not fit to bring him up. The courts will generally only make such an order in your favour if they are convinced that the mother is demonstrably unfit; for example if she is a drug addict or involved in prostitution or can find nowhere for herself and the baby to live.

You can also apply for a joint parental responsibilities order under the Family Law Reform Act 1987. This would give you equal rights with your ex-girlfriend regarding the care of your baby. It is anticipated that these orders will only be made with the consent of both parents and you must consider whether you can persuade your ex-girlfriend to give her consent. It is also anticipated that such orders are intended to cover situations where a couple live together as man and wife, in order that the co-habiting father may have the same rights as a father who is married to the child's mother. The final decision will be taken in the best interests of the child.

**My boyfriend and I have been living together for
three years and we have recently had a child.
What steps can we take to give my boyfriend a
legal status in relation to our child?**
You can apply for a 'joint parental responsibilities' order
in the magistrates' court which will give your boyfriend
equal rights with you to custody and the upbringing of
your child (see above). This will mean that you will share
parental rights in the same way as a married couple would
do.

To obtain a joint parental responsibilities order, you
may either go to the magistrates' court or, once the
Children Act is fully in force, you will be able to draw up
your own written agreement which you can have
approved by a solicitor without going to court.

**How do rights to custody and access affect the
payment of maintenance for a child?**
Not at all. If the parents of a child are married, then each
parent has a duty in law financially to maintain the child.
When a couple separate, the parent with custody (or
'residence' as it will become) will be entitled to a payment
of maintenance from the other, non-custodial parent so
long as his or her means permit this. In assessing the
capacity of a non-custodial parent to pay maintenance
towards a child's upbringing, the courts will disregard any
other financial liabilities which it considers non-essential
– for example, a non-custodial father who argues that he
is unable to pay because he has to make large payments
on an extravagant car will find his protests overruled. On
the other hand, where a non-custodial father has a new
family to support, these children will not take precedence
over his first family, but their needs will be taken into
account in assessing his ability to pay maintenance for his
first family. The court may not make an order which
reduces the father's income to below that of income

support, making him eligible for State benefits.

The award of custody or access does not affect the liability to contribute towards the maintenance of one's children. This is equally true in the case of unmarried parents. The proven father of a child born outside marriage has an obligation to support that child regardless of whether or not he is awarded parental rights or access (see above).

Do the procedures for applying for maintenance for a child born outside marriage differ from applications for maintenance payments towards keeping children of a marriage?

Since 1 April 1989, the same procedures apply to applications for maintenance of children whether or not the parents are married to one another. Applications can be made in either the magistrates', the county or the High Court. Orders made before this date for a child born outside marriage were known as 'affiliation' orders and could only be made in the magistrates' court. Any existing affiliation orders will continue to be known as such and any further applications, for example for variation, will be dealt with by the magistrates' court under the old law.

5: Local Authority Responsibilities for Children, Young People and Families

Local authorities (or councils) have been given the responsibility by Parliament of assisting children and young people who live in their areas when they or their families experience problems which may lead to the break-up of the family; these may be problems related to money, or to the children within the family, or to the adults. The departments within local authorities which have responsibility in these areas are Social Services, and to a lesser extent the Education Service. Because the attitude of the law is that children are entitled to special protection and consideration, local authorities are under a legal duty to promote the welfare of children by providing them and their families where possible with appropriate council services.

What types of assistance can children and young people in trouble expect from the local authority for the area in which they live?
These can include:
   (a) practical help with family services;
   (b) financial assistance;
   (c) accommodation for some children on a short-term basis ('voluntary care'), or other limited housing provision for homeless young people.
   All these services are dealt with in more detail below.
   Where family problems are more long-term, and any child (up to the age of 17) is not receiving the sort of care within the family that he or she is considered to need,

the local authority is empowered by law to remove legal parental responsibility from the parent or parents and effectively to transfer it to the authority's social workers. This usually happens only when the measures listed above have failed to improve the situation. It may be considered necessary for the local authority to remove the child from the family home on a permanent basis. This is known as 'taking the child into care', that is the care of the local authority, and is discussed in Chapter 6. Sometimes children or young people will need the local authority to intervene via the courts to remove them from the family home in an emergency, for example where they are in danger of physical or sexual abuse. This is discussed in Chapter 7.

How do I find out which local authority has responsibility for me?
You should contact your nearest town hall, where the offices of your local authority are based. They will ask you for your address (or your last permanent address) and direct you to the particular offices of the council which have responsibility for you (usually each local authority is divided up again into a number of 'catchment' areas). If the town hall you contact turns out not to be your local authority, give them your address and ask them which local authority has responsibility for you. They should be able to help.

Up to what age do local authorities have legal responsibilities towards children and young people living in their area?
At present, the law gives local authorities responsibility for all children and young people living in its area under the age of 18. Under the Children Act, the local authority will continue to have these responsibilities but only towards 'children in need'. These are defined as children

who have health or social development problems or disabilities who live in the local authority area; for example a child who suffers from an illness such as epilepsy or asthma, or who has a behavioural problem or learning difficulties at school, or is substantially and permanently handicapped by a disability (for example, blindness, loss of mobility, deafness). To prove this, you may need supporting letters from someone like a GP or a schoolteacher.

All the services listed above are available to children and young people living within the area up to the age of 18. This will generally remain the case under the new law in the Children Act 1989, although some services will be more difficult to get for over 16-year-olds (see below).

Are there any other qualifications for assistance?
This will depend upon the sort of help which you are asking for (see below). It will also depend upon how your local authority interprets its obligations to assist you, and how it decides to spend the money available to it from ratepayers and Central Government. Lack of available resources has sometimes been considered by the courts to be a sufficient reason for a council to refuse to help; if you are refused help in any of the circumstances outlined below, you should seek legal advice from one of the sources detailed in the final chapter of this book.

A. QUESTIONS FOR PARENTS

My children live at home with me and I wouldn't want them taken into care, even on a temporary basis. However, I do feel that I need some outside support in order to cope. What can the local authority do to help?
Local authorities are charged by Parliament with the responsibility to avoid the need to take children into residential care (that is, removing them from the care of

their parents and placing them in a children's home or with foster parents, generally at the local authority's expense). The ways the law envisages local authorities avoiding taking a child into care include the provision of appropriate family services such as help at home, child care facilities, counselling facilities via a family centre, and assistance to enable the family to take a holiday. The Children Act contains a detailed schedule listing the sort of services social workers may provide to help out under difficult circumstances without taking the children into care.

Once the Children Act is brought into effect, local authorities will be able to make charges for some (but not all) family services, as and when they feel that a family can afford to pay for them. Where services such as counselling or transport are provided for a young person over the age of 16 the young person him or herself may be asked to contribute towards the cost. Whether your local authority decides to charge you or not will depend upon the funds available in that area, your own means and the discretion of the social workers dealing with your case.

The Children Act places a duty on local authorities to provide after-school and holiday facilities for children living in their area who fall within the definition of children 'in need' (see above for the meaning of this term).

The Children Act will also enable a court in any family proceedings (including proceedings following a divorce or separation; see Chapter 4) to make a 'family assistance order'. This means that the local authority has a duty to allocate either a social worker or a probation officer to the child or children. A family assistance order can only be made with the consent of the child and adult concerned (that is, the person with whom the child lives), and will last for a maximum of 6 months. Throughout that period, the local authority must offer support to the child and his family and may require the adult with whom the child lives to undertake to keep the authority informed of the child's address, and allow the social worker to visit the child.

Many of my family's problems are money-related. Can the local authority do anything to help?

Yes. Local authorities may decide that the best way to help a family and to avoid the need for a child or young person to come into care is to offer financial assistance. This might be used, for example, to buy furniture or bedding for a child's room, to provide heating for unheated accommodation, or to buy essential equipment for a baby.

Funds are strictly limited and some councils allocate more money than others. The new Children Act introduces rules for any money payment to take the form of a loan if the local authority decides that you can afford to pay the money back at a later stage.

How can I persuade the local authority social worker that my family should qualify for family services and/or financial assistance?

Local authorities carry the responsibility of doing everything possible to avoid the need to take a child into care and hence break up a family. In practice, the sort of help that social workers can provide to avoid this happening and enable you and your family to cope at home is limited by available resources. On the other hand, remember that it costs the local authority much more in the long run to take your child into residential care than it would do to provide you with help and support at home. If you are determined to keep your family together at home you should tell your social worker this and ask for the services described above.

I don't want my children taken into care permanently, but I cannot look after them properly at the moment. Can the local authority do anything to help?

Yes. The local authority, via your social worker, can offer what used to be known as 'voluntary care'.

Sometimes the best way to relieve pressure on a family with problems is for one or more of the children to be taken into the temporary care of the local authority.

Under childcare law dating from the early 1980s, this has become known as 'voluntary' care. Unless the whereabouts of the child's parents are not known, this arrangement takes place with their consent, or sometimes at their specific request. There is no need to go to court.

The agreement to provide voluntary care on a short-term basis can be worked out between yourself and a social worker. The local authority will provide your child with somewhere to live and will meet his other living costs – although you may be asked to contribute (see below). This arrangement should be designed to meet your needs and those of your child and may be ended at your request (see below).

Social workers have a duty to offer voluntary care to parents who are finding it difficult to cope for any good reason. For example, the local authority will be obliged to offer voluntary care if you (as a single parent) were admitted to hospital where there are no other relatives to take care of your child, or where you need time to sort out your own emotional problems and are unable properly to care for your child. In addition, the local authority is obliged to provide 'respite care' for handicapped or disabled children under special rules designed to give their families a break from the stress of caring for their special needs. Voluntary care is at present provided for around 50,000 children throughout England and Wales.

Under the new law in the Children Act, the expression 'voluntary care' will disappear but the local authority will continue to have a duty to accommodate children whose parents have abandoned them or are temporarily unable to care for them. Although the new law continues to place a duty on social workers to offer temporary accommodation for children away from the family home under such circumstances, you will also have to demonstrate that your child qualifies as a 'child in need' (that is, those with a health or development problem or a disability as discussed above).

At the moment, the duty to provide voluntary care extends up to the age of 17. After the Children Act is brought into force, if you are looking for accommodation away from your family home for a young person between 16 and 18 (for example, where a family with other younger children finds it difficult to support an older child who has left school but has no job), you will need in addition to convince social workers that the young person's welfare will be 'seriously prejudiced' if he or she is not provided with accommodation (this is not the same thing as showing that the rest of the family's welfare will otherwise be seriously affected). The separate question of housing for homeless young people is discussed below.

Remember that with all the residential options outlined above that this is a *voluntary* arrangement, you need not agree to anything you don't want to. You should also remember that your co-operation is essential if this temporary break is going to give you the relief from pressure that you need, for whatever reason. You should work out in advance what you need from the arrangement to make it work for the best, and what is important in order to maintain your relationship with your child, who will, it is anticipated at this stage, be returning home to live with you after the break.

Can I make private fostering arrangements for my child to see us through a difficult period?

Yes, but the local authority will have to be informed in order that they can oversee the arrangements you make. Under the Children Act, local authorities will have a legal responsibility to supervise private fostering arrangements. This will be effected by social workers making visits to private foster homes and satisfying themselves that the foster children are being properly cared for.

Can I be asked to contribute towards the cost of my child's upkeep whilst he is in care?

Yes. This is already the case under the existing law and is repeated in the new legislation. Up to the age of 16, the parents of a child may be asked (at the discretion of the local authority – councils vary in their policies) to contribute towards the cost of accommodating and maintaining him or her away from the family home. A contribution cannot be asked for where the parents are receiving income support or family credit (see Chapter 1).

Over the age of 16, the young person is liable to contribute instead of his or her parents. If the young person is working, a contribution may be taken from his or her wages; if unemployed, it will be taken from any state benefit payable to the young person.

What sort of rights does this voluntary arrangement give social workers and foster parents to make decisions about my child whilst he is in their care?

Under a voluntary arrangement of the sort described above, none of your rights as a parent of your child pass to the local authority (as they would do if a full care order were made, see Chapter 6). For example, you cannot be prevented from visiting your child whenever you want to. Parental access may be restricted (other than in emergencies, and then only for 7 days – see below) only where children are in 'full' care. While the arrangements for where your child will live are being worked out, you should try to establish some basic principles about access and other matters which concern you, for example when you should visit your child, whether you wish to be notified in case of any illness, etc. If your child is to be fostered, this may mean negotiating with the foster parents (see below).

Your consent remains necessary for your child to receive medical or dental treatment (if he or she is under 16); your permission is necessary for your child to go on a school trip under the care of teachers, or for your child to leave the country on a holiday. How you negotiate these and similar issues with the children's home or the foster parents caring for your child is a matter for you to decide.

What about emergencies?
Once your child is in the 'voluntary' care of the local authority, decisions that have to be made at short notice (for example, whether the child needs emergency treatment by a doctor following an accident) may be taken by the local authority, but they must consider the wishes of the child and the parents in doing so. To authorize emergency medical (or dental) treatment without the parents' consent, the authority must show that they have made efforts to contact the parents, but have failed.

The Children Act also gives local authorities a special dispensation to take decisions which in law should be the right of the parents, in circumstances where otherwise a member of the public might be injured.

The Children Act gives local authorities the power to restrict parental access to a child in voluntary care in an emergency where access might seriously affect the child's welfare; for example, where one parent has been charged with assaulting or abusing that child. This restriction may only last for 7 days and it must then be approved by the juvenile court if it is to be further extended.

An emergency may very occasionally arise where social workers feel that a child's behaviour is such that she should be placed in 'secure accommodation'. This should only happen where a child has a history of running away, and is in danger as a result, or where he or she is considered likely to cause 'significant' harm to others or him/herself unless placed in secure accommodation under supervision. After a maximum period of 72 hours the juvenile court will be asked to decide whether any of these grounds exist. If the court decides that such grounds do exist, an order may be made for a period of up to 3 months (and any order may be renewed for a further period on application). When such an order is made with respect to a child by virtue of a voluntary arrangement, the local authority will only accommodate the child in 'secure accommodation' but the parent (or the person with parental responsibility) may of course remove the child and take him home (subject currently to the provisions on notice; see below) at any time. Where the child is in 'full care' (see Chapter 6), either the parent or the child may appeal to the Crown Court against the making of the order.

How can I ensure that my child's case is regularly reviewed by the social workers responsible?

The present law gives every child being looked after by a local authority the right to a six-monthly review of his or her case. This should consider the future of the child and the course of action which is in his or her best interests. The child who is the subject of the review has the right to be kept informed of the progress of his or her case 'as far as is reasonably practicable'.

Will I be consulted about the review?

There is no legal right for you or your child to be present at such a review. The new law in the Children Act gives the Secretary of State the responsibility for laying down regulations in this area, but until this is done it is not possible to be sure how far they will go; it is likely that they will guarantee to parents and children the right to be consulted about the review.

There is no right either for you or your child to see the various reports and other paperwork which will be considered in the review. Many local authorities will now, as a matter of good practice, consult with both the child and the parent, admit them to the review and allow them to see all documentation.

Is there any formal mechanism for making a complaint to the local authority about any aspect of their handling of my child's case?

At present no, although some local authorities do have their own internal procedures. Under the Children Act, a formal mechanism which will apply to every local authority will be put into effect.

The Children Act requires every authority to establish a complaints procedure to investigate complaints made by any child or parent of a child in their care (whether full care, temporary care or a 'child in need' (see above). This procedure must also address any complaints brought by local authority foster parents. The authority will also have a duty to publicize its complaints machinery in order that you may, if you wish, take advantage of it. You should ask to see whatever literature the authority produces for this purpose.

The complaint will be considered by officers from the local authority concerned and at least one officer from another authority, who is expected to take an independent stance.

The manner in which your complaint will be investigated will be broadly determined by regulations drawn up by the Minister. These regulations have not yet appeared, but will oblige authorities to consult with the person making the complaint and seek the views of anyone else (for example, your child) who is involved in the case. Once the investigation of your complaint has been concluded, the authority must inform you (and your child, if old enough to understand the proceedings) of its decision on your complaint and the reasons for it.

What happens when I decide that I am ready to cope with my child returning home to live with me?

Since no legal rights have been transferred to the local authority, the arrangements outlined above may be ended at any time at your request. Under the existing law, if your child has been in voluntary care for 6 months or more you must give notice of 28 days in writing before you may remove him or her from the children's home or foster home. If your child has been in voluntary care for less than 6 months, you need give no notice at all, but usually it will be in the child's best interests to give some warning of your intention.

If the local authority is concerned about the welfare of the child if he or she returns to live with the family, this period of notice may be used by the local authority to explore the possibilities of obtaining a full care order on your child, to remove your legal rights permanently. In order to do this the local authority will have to show that you are in some way not able to give your child the care he or she needs, and you may contest this. The ways in which local authorities may take children into 'full' care (that is taking over your legal responsibility) are discussed in the next chapter.

Under the Children Act, which drops the label 'voluntary care', parents will not have to give any period of notice before removing their child from accommodation provided under a voluntary arrangement. The only exception to this is where the child has turned 16, when he or she will be allowed the final decision on whether to return home or continue to live in local authority accommodation. If a young person of 16 or over agrees to stay in local authority care, the parents cannot insist that he or she returns to the family home.

B. QUESTIONS FOR CHILDREN AND YOUNG PEOPLE

Where will I live while I am in voluntary care?
There are a number of different options as to where you live, and you should tell your social worker what you would prefer and ask, if possible, to see the different places available before you choose. Sometimes there may be little choice, at least at first and especially if you have come into voluntary care without much warning. Usually the choice will be between:

(a) a residential children's home, run either by the local authority or by a voluntary organization such as the National Childrens Homes. These are usually large town- or country-houses, often just one of a row of other houses in a street and looking no different. Some of the older children's homes are much larger and look more like 'institutions'. The number of children who live in a children's home varies between 3 and 50 children and there will be a corresponding number of social workers, some of whom will 'live in';

(b) a community home, which may also be run either by the local authority or a voluntary body, or in partnership between both. Community homes are generally larger than children's homes and cater for a broader age range. Also they usually provide some other services on the premises, for example (although less and less often) education, or a family support centre, or an intermediate treatment centre for young offenders. Like a children's home, a community home will be run by social workers, plus any other staff necessary to operate the other services on the premises;

(c) a short-term placement with foster parents. All local authorities have approved foster parents on their books with whom children may be boarded, sometimes at short notice and for longer or shorter periods of time. This will be a family home and, ideally, your foster parents will have children of their own of around your own age. If fostering is an option, you will be taken to meet possible foster parents by your social worker and you should tell him or her how you would feel about living there. Your feelings must be taken into account in making the placement, but remember that sometimes it will be worked out at short notice and the choice may be limited by this.

Will I carry on going to the same school?

That will depend on whether you are still living close enough to your previous school to be able to continue to attend. This may be something you take into account in telling your social worker where you would prefer to live. Your social worker has a legal duty to try to ensure that you can continue to attend the same school, and also that your placement is as close as possible to your family home to make it easier for your mother or father to visit you regularly. Your religious beliefs and any special dietary requirements must also be taken into account in finding you a suitable placement.

How often will I see my parents?

Your parents are still your parents in the eyes of the law, and this means that they may visit you whenever they like. However, they may feel that it is best only to see you at certain times of the day or week in order to allow you to settle down in your new home. If you ever want to see your parents or feel that you would like them to visit you more often, you should talk to your social worker about this. It may be that your mother or father need a break from the responsibility of looking after you in order to get over an illness, or stress, and in that case they may have their own reasons for choosing not to visit you as often as you might like. Remember that this is intended to be a temporary arrangement and try to come to an understanding between yourselves about what sort of access will work best for you all.

I have been told by my social worker that there is going to be a 'case conference' about me? What does this mean?
The local authority has the legal duty to review your case every six months. Your social worker and the residential workers from your children's home (or your foster parents) will be asked about how you are settling down and they will discuss the best way to continue to look after your interests.

Can I go to the case conference?
Some local authorities allow children to attend their own case conferences, or reviews, and others do not. If you really want to be there, you should say so. Even if you are not allowed to be present, your social worker should talk to you about how you feel about your placement and represent your views to the other people taking part in the review.

Sometimes social workers are happy to show children the files which are kept on them while they are in voluntary care and will give you the opportunity to contribute what you want to it. You should ask if you can see your file if you want to, but you may be turned down.

What if I decide that I want to go home to my own family?

If you feel strongly that you want to return home, you should tell your social worker this. It may be that your mother or father is not ready to be able to cope with you back at home yet, maybe because they are still recovering from illness or stress. Alternatively, your social worker may have reasons for believing that you would be better off staying at the children's home or the foster home for a while longer. If this seems to be the case, you should ask him or her to tell you why. Remember that it is your social worker's duty to act in your best interests and you must assume that he or she has your welfare at heart. You should ask your social worker to explain to you why they think as they do about what is best for you, and you should make your own views clear also (especially if they are different from the opinion of your social worker), so that they can be taken fully into account.

Does the council have any duty to provide me with housing if I am homeless?

Up to the age of 16, if you are homeless because you cannot live with your family for whatever reason, the local authority has a duty to accommodate you as described above. After 16, that duty only applies where you can show that otherwise your welfare would be 'seriously prejudiced', or where you qualify under the Homeless Persons Act 1977 (see also *The Homeless Persons Handbook* published in this series).

Councils have legal duties under the Homeless Persons Act 1977 to provide homeless people living in their area with temporary housing under certain circumstances. You may qualify if you can show the following:

(a) that you are genuinely homeless. This may require your parents or anyone else with whom you have lived to put in writing the reasons why you can no longer live in their home;

(b) that you are not 'intentionally' homeless. For example, if you have given up accommodation or been evicted for non-payment of rent or for nuisance, you may be judged to have made yourself 'intentionally homeless'. This decision will be made in the first instance by your local Housing Department and if you are classified as 'intentionally homeless' you should seek further advice from a law centre or Citizens' Advice Bureau;

(c) that you have a 'local connection', that is you live or work or have family associations in that area;

(d) that you have a 'priority need'. Even if you qualify under the grounds above, you stand very little practical chance of being accommodated unless you are considered to be someone with a 'priority need'. A person with priority need includes anyone living with dependent children, pregnant young women, or sometimes young people judged to be 'in danger of financial or sexual exploitation' (from the Code of Guidance which accompanies the Act).

If you cannot show that you have a 'priority need' the council is obliged only to offer you 'advice and assistance' with finding accommodation.

6: Going Into Care

Where social workers have been involved for some time with giving a family support such as that described in Chapter 5 or, occasionally, where an emergency arises (see Chapter 7), a decision may be made that the best way to protect the children in a family is to take them into full care.

In the majority of cases, this decision will be taken by social workers after alternative solutions have been tried – for example, the provision of family support services, or a period of 'voluntary care' or temporary accommodation (see Chapter 5). Where the situation with regard to any children of the family does not show any improvement after a period of time and gives cause for concern over the safety, health or general development of the children, social workers may feel that the children's long-term interests (particularly where they are still very young) make it essential to consider options such as fostering or adoption by another family.

What does the law mean when it talks of 'taking a child into care'?
By taking a child into 'full care' the local authority takes over the legal rights of a parent in relation to that child. This allows the local authority social workers instead of the natural parents, to take all major and day-to-day decisions about the child (for example, where he should live, with whom, where he should attend school, and so on). The only parental right which is left to the parent is the right to object to their child's adoption and generally, a presumption of access (see also below).

The decision to attempt to take a child into full care

will be taken by social workers in a case conference. However, the social workers alone cannot authorize this step. At present, to secure a full care order they must either apply for an order to a magistrate (or panel of magistrates) sitting in the juvenile court, or a committee of social services officers (to include senior managers) must meet and decide to pass a 'resolution' giving the local authority parental rights to the child.

Despite the different names and different procedures of these two 'routes into care' as they are known, both a care order and a resolution have exactly the same effect in law i.e. to make the local authority the child's legal parent. The transfer of parental rights and duties to the local authority continues either until the order is 'discharged' (see below) or until the child's 18th birthday, when it automatically lapses.

Under the new law in the Children Act 1989, this procedure will become greatly simplified. Instead of two 'routes into care', via either a care order in the juvenile court or a resolution passed by the social services committee, the new law will stipulate that only magistrates have the legal authority to take a child into full care. Social services committees will no longer have the legal power to commit a child into care.

What sort of arguments must the social workers make to persuade the magistrates (or, presently, the social services committee) that a child would be better off in full care?
There are a number of 'grounds' within childcare legislation currently in force on which social workers must base their arguments for taking a child into full care. At least one of these grounds must be proved to the satisfaction of the court of the committee.

The most commonly used ground is that the child is not developing, in terms of his or her health or emotional well-being, as it is expected that a child of a similar age should develop, and that this is due in some way to the inadequacy of the care he or she receives at home. To prove this, social workers will have to ask for the opinion of 'experts' in child development, such as the health visitor, or possibly a child psychiatrist or children's doctor, to confirm their own views formed from observing the family over a period of time. It may also be argued that the child is being ill-treated at home, and evidence of physical abuse will almost always result in a full care order being made.

Care orders may also be made where the child is a persistent non-school-attender or has been convicted of an offence.

When an order is being sought from the magistrates, the local authority must show not only that one of the grounds is satisfied but in addition that the child in question is in need of 'care and control' which he will not receive unless a full care order is made.

A social services committee resolution assuming parental rights may be passed where a child has been in 'voluntary care' (see Chapter 5) for three years. If this ground is used, no other evidence of problems in the family home is necessary, but the committee must believe that a resolution is in the child's best interests. Other grounds which may be used include 'the habits or mode of life of the parents' being unsuitable; orders have been made where the parent is a prostitute, or an alcoholic, or a drug addict. Failure to show one's children love and affection or take any real interest in them (for example, where the parents of young children in 'voluntary care' showed no interest in the children, and demonstrated no parental affection towards them when the children visited them at home) has also provided the basis for resolutions in a small number of cases.

The Children Act 1989 replaces all the different

grounds which can currently be used with just one condition which the local authority must prove in the juvenile court. Proceedings will no longer be conducted by social services committees. The new ground states that a care order may be made where the child has suffered, or is likely in the future to suffer 'significant harm' (whether physical, emotional, or other) as a result of the standard of parental care they are receiving. So in future two things will have to be proved to the satisfaction of the magistrates before making a care order:

(a) that the child has suffered or is in danger of suffering 'significant harm'; *and*

(b) that the parents' standard of care is below that 'reasonably expected' from a parent and that this standard of care is responsible for the situation which is causing concern.

What sort of 'proof' do the magistrates look for before making an order?

The magistrates or (at present) the committee which hears the social worker's case must be satisfied 'on the balance of probabilities' that the facts are as they are claimed to be. What this means in practice is that the magistrates and the committee accept that many elements of the case may be disputed. Where a parent disputes the facts presented by the social workers, the magistrates have to decide who they are most convinced is acting in the child's best interests.

In some cases, proof of certain events such as the mother's alleged drug-taking, or the father's alleged alcoholism, will be central to the local authority's case. It is for the magistrates to decide in each case whether they have enough factual 'proof' to make an order, where it is felt that the order would be in the child's long-term interest.

A. QUESTIONS FOR PARENTS

Will I receive an official notice from the local authority of its intention to take my child into full care?

Not always, under the present law (this will change when the Children Act is brought fully into effect; see below). While the local authority is going to the juvenile court to ask for a full care order (which will become the only 'route into care' under the new law in the Children Act), you as the parent must be given 14 days' notice of the hearing taking place. What you will receive through the post (or sometimes 'served' to you in person by a local authority officer) is a notice from the juvenile court telling you where the hearing will take place and setting a date for the hearing. It will state the section of which Act the local authority will be basing its case on. That section will correspond to one of the grounds described above.

If you have received this notice and wish to oppose the care order being made, you should take this notice to a solicitor. He or she will be able to tell you, from the notice, which ground or basis is being used for the local authority's application and you can then plan your defence, or counter-arguments.

If the local authority decides under the present law to take the decision to assume your parental rights in a social services committee, then you have no legal right to be informed in advance of the committee meeting. Some local authorities, as a matter of good practice, inform parents in advance. Sometimes through your own talks with the social worker you may know informally that the authority is planning to take such a step. In any case, you have no right to take any part in that meeting. The local authority does have a legal obligation to inform you within 14 days of the meeting that the decision has been made. You may then if you wish write back lodging your objection to the decision. If you do this, there must be a juvenile court hearing within 14 days to decide the matter and you will have an opportunity then to put forward your side of the story.

Under the Children Act, all proceedings to take a child into care will take place in the juvenile court, and you will be entitled to be informed in advance. Regulations to be made by the Secretary of State under the Act will determine the sort of notice you will receive.

Can I have a solicitor to represent me in court?

Yes. If you have consulted a solicitor about opposing the local authority's application to the court for a care order, or want to appeal against a social services committee resolution, you will probably want him or her to represent you at the court hearing. This means that he or she will put your case to the court and ask any friends, relations or other professionals who might support your case to give their view to the court (this entails calling them as witnesses).

Obviously the solicitor's time costs money. You may be entitled to legal aid to pay for all or part of the solicitor's costs. You should ask your solicitor to assess your income for the purposes of legal aid and to give you as clear an idea as possible (it is often difficult to be precise about how much work a case will involve at its outset) about how much it might cost you. See also Chapter 10, 'Getting Legal Advice and Representation'.

My child is too young to express an opinion over where or with whom she wants to live. Does this give me the right to speak on her behalf?

Not necessarily. There are times where the law recognizes that the parents' wishes and interests are not necessarily identical with what is in the long-term best interests of the child. Whether this is the case will depend upon surrounding considerations, such as the age of the child (for example, an older child is seen as more likely to be able to form an independent judgement) and the sort of relationship the parent has had with the child in the past and in the present.

Increasingly, where the child expresses a view over where he or she wants to live which is contrary to that of the parent, or where the parent is clearly unable to form an objective view of what is best for the child in the long term, or where a very young child who cannot express a view is involved, the magistrates hearing an application for a full care order will order that the child is represented in court separately from the parent. Some magistrates take the view that in cases where the child seems torn between the options, separate representation is essential to ensure that a solicitor's time and duty is committed wholly to the child as 'client' and is not similarly torn. This will better enable the child's best interests to emerge.

If your child is separately represented by a solicitor, the solicitor will appoint a 'guardian *ad litem*' to work with him or her. The guardian will be a social worker from another local authority (not the one applying for the care order against you) whose task is to befriend your child and interview him or her and any other relevant people about what might be the best outcome of the case. This view will then be expressed to the court at the hearing.

The guardian's view is often conclusive in care proceedings. It is as likely to go for you as against you. It is intended to be an independent judgement by another professional on what your local authority is suggesting as the best for your child.

My child has said that he doesn't want to live with me any more and he has told the social worker this too. Does this mean that I can't argue against the local authority in court?

No. Obviously if your child is considered to be sufficiently mature to reach a considered decision over where he lives, the court will place some weight upon this and it will admittedly make it very much more difficult for you and your solicitor to argue against a care order. Even if your child is very young, any opinion which he expresses will be taken into account by the court, which is after all there to determine his or her 'best interests'. This does not mean that the child's view will necessarily be decisive; for example, the court may interpret past events differently from the child.

Who else can talk to the court on my behalf – for example, can my child's grandmother or aunt or a family friend or neighbour tell the court that my child is best left at home with me?

Yes. The court may now hear from anyone who is accepted to have a relevant interest in your child's future. This includes grandparents but also any other 'significant' adults. If you want to ask your supporters to give evidence to the court, you should inform your solicitor and he or she will arrange for their evidence to be heard by the magistrates.

What sort of questions will the magistrates ask me in court?

First, you should expect your solicitor to go through the questions you may be asked with you before the hearing takes place, in order to prepare you. Tell your solicitor that you want to spend some time on this, once the sort of evidence the local authority will be bringing has become clear (your solicitor will have received copies of all the local authority reports on your child's case prior to the hearing).

No one would deny that giving evidence to a court may be a nerve-racking experience, especially if you are unfamiliar with the process. Most magistrates do try to make the atmosphere in the court as informal and relaxed as possible, and are sympathetic towards parents who are unused to court procedures and will try to put you at your ease.

Your own solicitor will question you first and you should have rehearsed this part already. The questions will relate to your care of your child, your management of the problems which have occurred, and how you now want the court to resolve the case. Then your child's solicitor (if there is one) will question you about the evidence given by the 'guardian' (above) and any other part of the local authority's case which is central to the issue of whether you can properly care for your child. Finally the solicitor for the local authority will question you about the evidence relied upon by the authority in applying for an order. For example, if the social worker has said that you have failed to ensure that your child attends school, you should explain why this has happened. Or if you have an alcohol or drug problem, you should tell the magistrates what steps you are taking to deal with it. If you feel that any of the evidence presented by the local authority is unfair, you should say so and why. The magistrates may ask you questions too, if they want clarification of anything you say during your testimony. Try to present your evidence calmly and unhurriedly; the court will have to wait for you.

On what basis will the magistrates make up their minds?

To make an order in any case, the magistrates must feel convinced that the 'ground' (see above) alleged by the local authority is supported by satisfactory evidence. But this is just the first part of the decision-making process. Next, the court has to agree that the child is in need of 'care and control' which he or she will not receive unless the care order is made. The final decision on whether or not to make an order should then be made according to what the magistrates see as the child's 'best interests'.

What sort of orders can the magistrates make?

If the magistrates decide that the 'ground' is proved to their satisfaction, they may still consider a full care order to be inappropriate. They may feel, for example, that this is too drastic a step and may instead prefer to leave your child at home with you but subject to a 'supervision order'.

A supervision order can last for up to three years and makes a particular local authority officer (for example, the family social worker, a probation officer, or an education social worker) responsible for monitoring your child's behaviour and the home situation (see also Chapter 3). Your child will have to see the supervision officer regularly or the local authority will take you back to court. You have no obligation to see the supervision officer yourself but he or she may from time to time ask to speak with you and it may be in your interests to develop an understanding between yourselves, as two people concerned about your child's welfare.

Occasionally magistrates hear an application for a full care order from social workers who have clearly not been able to prepare all the information they wanted to present to the magistrates in time for the hearing. In such cases the magistrates may feel sympathetic towards the local authority's view that a care order is necessary to protect the child but are unable to make an order because of the lack of evidence available. In such a case the magistrates may make an 'interim care order', which will temporarily transfer parental rights to the local authority but only until the necessary evidence can be brought before the court and a full hearing takes place. While an interim order is in force, the court may order either that your child lives with you or in a local authority placement.

If you feel that the local authority are taking too long to prepare their full case and that this delay is adversely affecting you and/or your family, you should complain to your family social worker. Some families whose cases were left unresolved in this way for months or even years have won a ruling from the European Court of Human Rights that this treatment violates their human rights. Under the Children Act, interim orders will only be allowed to run for 8 weeks.

Can we appeal against the making of a care order?

Appeal lies to the Crown Court. Appeal is possible both in your own right as a parent, and by or on behalf of your child. However you should be warned that the grounds on which appeals are considered are very narrow.

The care order may also be discharged before it is due to lapse (on your child's 18th birthday) on your (or your child's) application to the juvenile court. The court will discharge the order if it is 'appropriate' to do so but may substitute a supervision order (above). If the local authority make clear their intention to appeal against a discharge of a care order or supervision order granted by the juvenile court, the court may order the original order to subsist in the meantime, attaching particular conditions (for example your child may be able to return home to live with you, but will remain technically 'in care' until the appeal by the local authority is resolved).

If my child is taken into full care, where will he live?

In any one of the three residential options outlined for voluntary care (see Chapter 5). Children who are in care on a longer-term basis are more likely to be placed with foster parents than those in care for a brief temporary period.

Will I have any say in my child's life once he is in full care?

In law, you will no longer have any right to intervene in decisions taken about your child's life. In practice, if you can establish a good relationship with your child's social worker you may be given some say, or at least be consulted on major decisions.

In relation to your child's religious upbringing, the local authority has a duty in law not to place him anywhere (either to live or to be educated) which prevents him from continuing in the same faith. For example, dietary requirements for Muslim children must be respected, and children from Jewish families must be found a placement where they can, if they wish, continue to observe the Jewish Sabbath.

Will I be able to visit my child?

This will lie within the discretion of the social workers working on your child's case, although the Children Act gives a presumption of 'reasonable access' to every parent whose child is in full care. If you have been told that you cannot visit your child, you may appeal against this decision to the juvenile court. The magistrates will expect you to tell them how and why you feel that you and your child will benefit from continued access. Once this part of the Children Act is in force, the local authority will have to defend in court any decision to limit or remove your right to 'reasonable access'.

The social worker has told me that my child's foster parents want to adopt him. Do I have to agree?

No. The one parental right you retain after your child has been taken into care is the right to consent to, or to refuse, your child's adoption.

If the local authority feels strongly that adoption is the best course for your child, it may apply to a court to give it permission to go ahead without your permission. This is only granted in exceptional circumstances and is discussed further in Chapter 8.

My home situation has completely changed since my child went into care. Can I now get the care order lifted in order that he can come home to live with me?

Yes, you can go back to the magistrates in the juvenile court and ask them to discharge the order. You will have to explain how your circumstances have changed since the original order was made and persuade the magistrates that your child now has a future with you.

You would be well-advised to talk to the social worker(s) responsible for your child before applying for a discharge. If they agree that the care order should be lifted you will stand a good chance of persuading the magistrates that this is the proper course.

Under the Children Act, magistrates who discharge a care order will be able to make a range of other orders to regulate future arrangements at home. This might have the effect of making magistrates more willing to discharge care orders since they can continue to monitor the home situation through, for example, the use of residence and contact orders (see Chapter 4). For example, they may discharge the care order but make a residence order specifying with whom the child should live and a contact order specifying who may and who may not have access to him (for example, a violent father or mother's boyfriend could be excluded).

For information on the types of accommodation provided by local authorities for children in care, including the use of 'secure accommodation', see Chapter 5.

B. QUESTIONS FOR CHILDREN AND YOUNG PEOPLE

Will I be asked to appear in court and what sort of questions will I be asked?

Depending upon your age and what the magistrates consider to be your understanding of the case, you may be asked to be in court and answer questions put to you by the solicitors and the magistrates.

You will be asked about your home life and your relationship with your parents, and what you think would be the best outcome to the case – whether you stay at home or go into care. If you are not sure, or confused about the alternatives, you should tell the court this.

Usually you will be expected to give your evidence 'live' in court. If you feel uncomfortable about giving evidence in front of any of the adults – your parents, social workers or any others – who will be present in the court, you may answer questions put to you via a video link set up in a room in a separate part of the court building.

Will I have my own solicitor, or anyone else, to explain to the court how I feel?

If the magistrates are told that your views may be different from those of your parents, they may agree to a solicitor representing you separately. In order to pay for legal representation, you will be assessed for legal aid. This assessment is carried out according to your (not your parents') income and therefore it is almost certain that you will qualify.

If the court does not appoint a separate legal representative to put your views, you will 'share' your parents' solicitor.

If you do have your own solicitor, and possibly even if you do not, a 'guardian *ad litem*' will be appointed by the court to represent your interests. The guardian will be a social worker but from a different local authority than the one your own social worker is employed by. The guardian has the right to have access to all local authority records and reports on your case. The guardian will also talk to you about the circumstances which have preceded the authority's application for a care order and about how you feel now – for example whether you would rather stay at home or go into care, what makes it difficult to stay at home and anything else that seems to be relevant. Other people who have something to add will also be interviewed in order that the guardian may build up a full picture. He will then make a report to the court, drawing a conclusion about what outcome would be in your best interests. This report will be very influential when the magistrates come to make their decision.

Will I be allowed to remain in court when other people (my parents, for example) are being questioned?

Again, this will depend in the first place on your age and understanding. If you are allowed to listen to the other evidence, you might be asked by the magistrates to leave the court for a short time if certain evidence being given is not directly about you but hearing it may be hurtful or harmful to you; for example, the evidence given by your parents about one another.

Will I be allowed to see the reports my social worker/probation officer/education social worker/guardian *ad litem* write for the magistrates?
Yes, this is your right. However, anything written in the reports which is considered to be hurtful or harmful to you (see above) may be withheld from you.

If I am taken into full care, will I be allowed to decide where I live?
That will depend upon the options available in your local authority (see Chapter 5). You should express a view if you have one and your social worker must try to find you a placement as close as possible to your family home, to allow you to continue if possible to attend your old school, and stay within reach of your friends.

What if I don't like the children's home or foster home my social worker finds for me?
You should tell your social worker how you feel and explain why. You can't force the authority to move you but you can, and should, make your feelings clear. Sometimes the authority may be able to move you but not straight away in which case you must try to be as patient as possible.

Under the Children Act there is a new complaints procedure which you can use if you feel that your views have been disregarded. Many local authorities already have informal procedures you can use to make a complaint. Get details from NAYPIC (see Chapter 10 'Getting legal advice and representation').

What if I don't want my parents to visit me, or if I want my parents to visit me more often?
If you want to change the access arrangements with your parents you should tell your social worker and explain why. The local authority via its social workers has the

legal right to decide whether, and how often, your parents should be able to visit you. Again, if you are not satisfied with these arrangements you can make a complaint (see above).

What happens in relation to pocket-money and buying clothes and other things I need?

The residential social workers who run the home in which you live (or your foster parents) will give you pocket-money and the amount will be determined by the local authority itself. As you would expect if you were living at home, the rate varies according to age. Remember that it is the town hall and not your individual social worker who sets the rate!

The authority will also set a sum for buying you clothes and this will either be administered on your behalf or, depending on how old you are, you may be given your clothes allowance to manage for yourself.

I shall be 18 soon and my care order will lapse. I can't return home. Will the local authority help me to find somewhere else to live?

The local authority has no legal duty to accommodate you after you have turned 18. The authority does have a legal duty to continue to 'advise and assist' you if you were in care on your 16th birthday (so if you leave care before you are 16 you don't qualify for this help).

What sort of advice and assistance can I expect?

Most likely a social worker will be assigned to advise and counsel you. The Children Act stipulates that help may include assistance with expenses related to education, training or employment. If assistance is provided to enable you to undertake a course or training programme, this may continue until you are 21.

The authority may be able to offer you some (temporary) hostel accommodation. You may also be given some (limited) help with money, for example raising a deposit on renting a flat or a bedsit. The local authority may also be under a duty to provide you with accommodation if you are homeless (see Chapter 5).

The Children Act extends the right to receive 'advice and assistance' to young people who have spent three months or more in mental hospital and are now discharged.

How can local authorities act to protect children in emergency situations at home?

Where it is felt that a child is in danger of being physically or sexually abused, the law empowers the local authority, the police and children's welfare organizations, such as the NSPCC, to take emergency action to protect the child.

This is dealt with more fully in Chapter 7.

7: Emergency Protection for Children in Danger

Local authorities and other children's welfare organizations such as the National Society for the Prevention of Cruelty to Children, can act to protect children in an emergency when they appear to be at risk of physical, sexual or other abuse.

The effect of legal powers allowing local authorities and others (including the police) to intervene in these situations is to place the child who is considered to be in danger in the care of the authority (see Chapter 6), although in some cases this may only be a temporary measure while the cause of the danger is removed or minimized. For example, where a child has been sexually abused by a member of the same household, the abuser may be removed; or where the child has been subjected to physical ill-treatment from a family member, that person may receive counselling and other support, or be removed from the home altogether.

Recent tragic cases have highlighted the need for effective legal measures to allow children to be removed from the family home where they are at risk from abuse or violence. The effectiveness of the law depends at least in part upon the willingness of individuals inside and outside the family concerned to voice to the relevant authorities any well-grounded fears they might have over the safety of a particular child. This will be dealt with in more detail below. Equally important is that the law balances the safety of children with the long-term impact of separating them from their families, even for a short period of time.

How can local authorities act to protect children in an 'emergency'?

Where social workers feel that they have to act quickly in order to protect children in an 'emergency', the powers of the local authority to take children into care described in Chapter 6 are inappropriate. This is because it can take weeks or even months for social workers to gather the necessary evidence to bring care proceedings and to get a date fixed for a hearing before the magistrates. Since local authorities have obligations to protect children and young people living in their area from physical and sexual abuse, an alternative legal procedure may be used in an emergency. This allows the authority to remove the child from the family home by using a 'place of safety order' or, after the Children Act 1989 is brought into force, an 'emergency protection order' or a 'child assessment order' (see below).

At other times where abuse is suspected but not proved, the local authority may assign a social worker to visit a family regularly and be on the look-out for any visible signs of abuse (for example, marks or bruising) or signs of neglect (for example malnutrition) amongst the children.

Every local authority maintains an 'at risk' register to which the names of all children within the area are added when there is concern for their safety and protection. It is estimated that around 50,000 children are on at risk registers throughout England and Wales. A child's name may be added to the register following the expression of concern by someone who knows the child such as a teacher or a neighbour. Anyone who approaches the Social Services Department of a local authority with stated reasons for concern about the possible ill-treatment or neglect of a child living within that area should expect their intervention to be treated in confidence. What happens next has varied between different parts of the country, according to different local authority policies and resources. The local authority should investigate the allegations and in most authorities placing a child's name on the register will mean that a social worker will be assigned to the family and try to make regular visits.

When the Children Act comes into effect, for the first time local authorities will be under a legal duty to investigate any case notified to them where the child is at risk of serious harm, or where there is cause to suspect that the child may be in danger. This investigative duty includes the duty to ensure that the social worker put on the case gains access to the child, or if access is refused to take legal steps (see below) to ensure that the child is actually seen by the social worker for the purposes of the investigation.

The new law will both extend the duty of the local authority to take particular steps following notification of a child in possible danger or at risk and strengthen the powers of social workers to carry out visits in such circumstances.

How does the local authority obtain the legal right to remove children believed to be in danger from their homes?

When the local authority feels that it is necessary or a matter of urgency to remove a child from the family home, the present law allows them (or the police or the National Society for the Prevention of Cruelty to Children) to apply to a magistrate for a 'place of safety order'. The reason for the application is usually that the authority fears that the child is in danger of physical or sexual abuse. The hearing to decide whether the order will be made takes place before a single magistrate without the parents (or whoever the child lives with) or the child being present. This is known as an *ex parte* ('without the parties') hearing.

The magistrate who hears the case must decide whether the child is in danger of abuse or further abuse if he or she is not removed from the family home. Effectively, the magistrate is being asked to decide whether the local authority would be successful if they applied at a later date (giving them time to get all the necessary evidence together) for an order taking the child or young person permanently into their (i.e. local authority) care (see Chapter 6). This is to ensure that children are not removed on an emergency basis from their family home without very careful scrutiny of the circumstances.

Under the Children Act, place of safety orders are renamed 'emergency protection orders'. It is envisaged that applications for emergency protection orders (known as EPOs) will be made by officers of either local authorities or the National Society for the Prevention of Cruelty to Children (NSPCC).

The magistrate can decide to make an EPO on one of two grounds:

(a) that the child is likely to suffer significant harm if he or she is not removed from the family home (this is effectively a decision on whether the local authority could, at a later date, obtain a full care order on this child; see Chapter 6), or, exceptionally, if he or she is not left in the care of the local authority, but instead returned to the family home. This includes considerations about possible 'future harm' (see Chapter 6) and so an EPO may be grounded on fears about the child's future safety. It is intended that this will enable orders to be made in situations where there are strong grounds for concern, but before any actual abuse takes place (see also below, under 'wardship');

(b) that, having made inquiries, an 'authorized person' (an officer of the local authority or the NSPCC) has been refused access to the child and believes that it is a matter of urgency that the access to the child should take place in order to assess the validity of concerns about the child's safety. This may mean that the court has little or no actual evidence before it of the possibility of 'significant harm' (above) but will still be able to make an order empowering social workers to insist on access to the child and, if necessary, to take the child away from home for assessment.

In making an EPO, the court may also make an order that the child should be subject to medical and/or psychiatric examination. Because the legal effect of the EPO is to transfer parental rights to the local authority (or the NSPCC), the permission of the parent of the child is not required for such an examination to take place. If the child is considered to be sufficiently mature to give 'informed consent', he or she may refuse consent to being examined, in which case no examination may take place. Until the new law comes into effect it is not clear at what age the courts will generally consider children capable of giving 'informed consent'.

In addition, under the Children Act a child may be removed on the order of a magistrate for up to seven days for assessment by social workers, child psychologists and doctors. This is to be known as a child assessment order. It is intended to be used where a social worker has had difficulty seeing the child, for example gaining entry to his or her home, but where the grounds (above) for securing an EPO transferring parental rights do not exist.

A child assessment order will require the parents or whoever is responsible for the child to bring him forward for the purpose of assessment. Assessment may take place at home, or in a hospital or clinic, and the child may be away from home for some or all of this period. Since this may involve a medical and/or psychiatric examination, once again the child may in some circumstances be entitled to refuse consent (above). Because parental rights do not pass when a child assessment order is made, any examination would require the consent of the child's parent if he or she is under 16 years old. The effective use of assessment orders, then, envisages some degree of co-operation between the child's family and social services and in this important respect their operation is likely to differ from EPOs (above).

Details of the procedure to be followed in court when considering making these orders will be outlined in regulations to be made by the Secretary of State under the Children Act.

Does the law give any special powers to the police to intervene in cases of suspected abuse?

The third and final means by which the Children Act will enable the authorities to remove children in cases of emergency is by giving new powers to the police. This will be known as 'police protection' and allows the police to remove a child from home for up to 72 hours, by which time the police should have informed the relevant local authority and conducted an investigation into the circumstances of the case. Where it appears that the child would continue to be in danger at home, the local authority will take over the case and apply for an EPO or child assessment order (see above).

How in practice will the new law enforce emergency provisions for the removal of children where the family refuse to allow social workers into the home?

The Children Act includes a number of new provisions designed to address this problem. The new law will allow the court which makes an emergency protection order to issue a warrant (such as is issued by a magistrate giving police officers the right to enter private homes for other purposes, for example searching for stolen goods) which will give the right to a police-officer (usually accompanied by the social worker) to enter the family home in order to gain access to that child or children.

If the magistrate believes that any person is concealing information about the child's whereabouts then the emergency protection order can include a requirement that this person disclose any relevant information. If this person still refuses to reveal the vital information, he or she could be prosecuted for contempt of court.

The Children Act makes it an offence to obstruct the implementation of an EPO, and to abduct a child who is the subject of an EPO or in police protection.

Am I obliged to allow my child to be examined by a doctor before the emergency order is made?

No. You may refuse to allow your child to be examined (for example, to look for signs of neglect or ill-treatment) since this is your right as parent before any legal order has been made. However, where the authority believes there to be good reason to suspect that your child has been abused, your refusal to allow a medical examination to take place may lead them to apply for an EPO which will give them the legal right to order an examination.

How long can an emergency order last?

At present, if the magistrate decides to make a place of safety order, it will last for up to 28 days (or 8 days where the child is less than 10 years old). Under the Children Act, an emergency protection order will last for 8 days in all cases, but may be extended (but only on the application of a local authority, the police or the NSPCC, and not by any other member of the public) for another 7 days. The emergency order may be extended only once.

Although the total length of time for which an order may last is therefore significantly reduced under the new legislation, if at the end of the 15 day period it is felt that the child would be in danger if he or she were allowed to return home, the local authority may apply for an interim or a full care order (see below).

An assessment order (see above) may last for a maximum of 7 days.

Who does the law regard as exercising parental rights once an emergency order is made?

The effect of an EPO being made in favour of the local authority (or NSPCC) is to give the local authority (or NSPCC) responsibility for the child as if it were the child's legal parents. This clears up what has been a confused legal position in relation to place of safety orders (above) which did not give parental rights to the authority but were often treated in practice as if they did. Under the new law the authority has the right to make a number of decisions on behalf of your child as if it were your child's legal parent.

In the case of a child assessment order, the authority does not acquire parental rights (above). Where a child is in 'police protection' (above) the police do not acquire any parental rights to take decisions about the child, but instead have the legal duty to safeguard the child's welfare.

Where will my child be accommodated if an emergency order has been made?

The first decision which will be made by a local authority successful in obtaining an emergency protection order is where the child is to live for the duration of the order. This will usually be either in a children's home or with foster parents. Occasionally the order may specify the emergency placement as being the children's ward of a local hospital.

If the order is for assessment only, your child may continue to live at home during the seven days of the assessment period, or he or she may be away for some or all of that time. If you feel that it is practical for your child to continue to live at home and visit the hospital or clinic for assessment during the daytime, you should make this clear to the social worker.

Will I be allowed to visit my child after he has been taken away under an emergency order?

The second decision the local authority will make will be whether or not to allow the parents of the child access to visit him or her while the order is in force. At present, the authority is not given any instructions on the question of access by the magistrate who made the order. If the local authority decide that you should not be allowed to visit, you may appeal against this to the juvenile court, i.e. a hearing before magistrates at which you may appear and put your case. You may wish to consult a solicitor about this, and arrange for someone to represent you at the hearing (see Chapter 10 'Getting legal advice and representation').

When the Children Act becomes law, a local authority which has obtained an EPO will be obliged by law to allow the parents of the child reasonable access to their child whilst the order is in force. If the local authority believes that parental access is not in the child's interests, the magistrate making the original order may be asked to order that there should be no or limited access. If such a condition is attached to the order, the parents may appeal to the juvenile court, against the decision to restrict or curtail their access, as above. Similarly, a child who is in 'police protection' must be allowed to see his or her parents unless the police officer responsible for the case feels that this is not in the child's interests.

Once an emergency order has been made, what happens next?

Once a child has been taken into care under an emergency order, the local authority must fully investigate the circumstances which led to the order being made and determine what further action will best serve the child's interests. Under the Children Act, authorities are placed under a specific legal duty to investigate what course of action will best protect the child once an emergency order has been made.

This may mean that social workers negotiate with the family and decide that it is safe for the child to return home under close supervision, i.e. regular visits and family counselling. In this case, the order will either expire without renewal (see above), or may be discharged on the application of the authority at an earlier date. In some cases the child may return home while the order is still in effect, for example in a situation where the suspected abuser has agreed to move out of the family home.

In other cases, subsequent scrutiny of the family situation may lead social workers to believe that it remains unsafe for the child to return home. In this case, the order may be renewed (although under the Children Act renewal will be limited to once only) or a new order may be substituted in its place. Most commonly the order substituted in place of an emergency order is an interim care order. This will be granted on the application of a local authority where the magistrates feel convinced that there is sufficient evidence to justify the authority retaining legal care of the child, and that there is a good chance that in time sufficient evidence will have been gathered to allow them to apply for a full care order.

The hearing for an interim order will take place with all parties present before the magistrates in the juvenile court. The parents of the child and the child himself have the right under the Children Act to make representations to the court.

At present, local authorities may obtain interim orders for up to 6 months and may renew the interim order again and again. This has meant that sometimes cases have taken months or even years to be finally resolved, whether or not a full care order can or should be made. Under the Children Act, an interim order will last for only 8 weeks. At the end of that time the local authority must present its full case for a care order and the magistrates will make a ruling (see also Chapter 6).

I have read of children being removed from their parents in emergencies after being made 'wards of court'. What does this mean?

In some cases where it is not possible to obtain a place of safety order (for example, where the case cannot be heard at once, or where the evidence is not clear), local authorities or any other individual convinced that a child is in danger may apply to the High Court in London for the child to be made a 'ward of court'.

The High Court will ward a child where the judge is convinced that the child is in need of protection. The evidence is not considered in the same degree of detail and scrutiny as is required for a place of safety order. Similarly, where a place of safety order is due to expire and there is insufficient evidence to obtain an interim order (see above) the local authority may decide instead to apply for wardship.

The effect of wardship is that the High Court, rather than the local authority, becomes the child's parent in law. Usually 'care and control' (that is, the day-to-day organization of the child's life) is delegated by the High Court to the relevant local authority. The High Court must be consulted on major decisions such as whether the child should return home at any point.

The use of wardship in this way by local authorities to 'fill gaps' in the present law has been widely criticized. The Children Act gives local authorities wider powers to act in emergencies (see above) in order that they need not have recourse to the High Court. It also prevents local authorities from using wardship where they could use a statutory power such as an application for an emergency order to achieve the same result.

I have found out that a member of my household has been abusing my child, who has been removed under an emergency order. The social worker has told me that my child cannot come home until this person has left. What can I do?
There are a number of steps you can take, with the assistance of the local authority, to exclude that person from your home and enable your child to be returned home to you.

You may be able to persuade that person that they can no longer live with you and if they accept this you may not need recourse to legal action to exclude them. If this is not possible you may need to apply to the magistrates' (or county) court for an order prohibiting them from entering your home and assaulting either you or your children (or any other children who live with you, such as foster children, or the children of a relative). This is called an 'exclusion order'.

Exclusion (or 'ouster') orders are available to unmarried women against their living-in partners (in the county court) and to married women against their spouses (in the county court or magistrates' court). To grant an order the court must be convinced that there is a present or imminent danger of physical or sexual abuse to you or any children living with you unless this person is excluded from your home. If the local authority has become involved with your case and in particular where your children have been removed under an emergency order (even if it has expired) you can expect help from your social worker in obtaining such an order. For example, you can expect your social worker to come to court and testify on your behalf about the circumstances which make it necessary for this person to be excluded from the home.

If an exclusion order is granted, it will be for a limited period of time (usually three months). If the person who has been excluded breaks the order (known as an 'injunction') during that time, you should inform the police immediately. If the order has been made by the magistrates with a 'power of arrest' attached, the police will be empowered to arrest this person if he breaks the order and enters your home. Therefore it is very important that the magistrates are asked to attach a power of arrest to any exclusion order which they make. If no power of arrest has been attached, it may prove more difficult to persuade the police to intervene. If this is the case and you have evidence that the order has been broken you should return to the court and ask for a power of arrest to be added to the original order to ensure that any future breaches will result in arrest.

If the court is not prepared to make an exclusion order they may instead make an order prohibiting the named person from assaulting you or your children in future. This will allow them to go on living in your home but may be enforced in the same way as an exclusion order (above) if it is broken.

In some cases the police may wish to take direct action against the alleged abuser, i.e. by prosecuting him for assault. To an extent this decision will depend upon whether you feel that this person should be prosecuted, since in practice the police will find it difficult to bring sufficient evidence for a successful prosecution without your co-operation. Sometimes the police may feel that a prosecution should go ahead regardless, in which case you may be compelled to come to court and give evidence in court against this person.

What sort of follow-up care such as personal counselling is available for family members after abuse has been discovered?

Neither the local authority nor the child welfare organizations who have become involved in your case are under any legal duty to provide counselling or any other follow-up facility. However, many authorities will do so if you ask. Even where your authority does not have the expertise to provide family counselling it is always possible for you to be referred to professionals based in another authority, or in a hospital, or a private organization. Although the authority has no mandatory duty to bear the costs of such counselling, you should argue that counselling is essential to enable you to keep your family together after the trauma of abuse being discovered. Every local authority has a legal duty to take whatever steps are necessary to keep families together and prevent the need to take children into care (see Chapter 5). Moreover, the Children Act recommends that every authority should have access to professional counselling facilities and that they should publish a list of the services they can provide to families in need.

8: Adoption

The previous three chapters of this book described the way in which local authority Social Services Departments can provide temporary or permanent accommodation (in local authority children's homes or with foster parents) for children who cannot live with their natural families for whatever reason.

This chapter looks at the process of adoption of a child by a new family. Local authority care can provide a short- or medium-term solution where the problems preventing the family from living together can be addressed and the children returned within a few weeks or months. Where the problems are long-term, and it becomes clear that it will not be possible for a child to be brought up by his own parents, it may be necessary to look beyond local authority care to a more permanent solution in the interests of the child's long-term welfare and stability. Local authorities have legal responsibilities to find for children who are in long-term care adoptive families who can take over their care on a long-term basis and provide them with a permanent home.

Not all adoption placements are arranged by local authorities (although all prospective adoptions must be approved by the Social Services Department; see below). Sometimes adoption takes place within an extended family – for example, an aunt and uncle, or grandparents may take over the care of a child where the parents have died, are working abroad, are serving a term in prison, or are otherwise unable to bring up their child themselves.

What is the effect of an adoption order?
The law of adoption allows one or two adults other than

123

the child's natural parents to take over parental rights. From the point at which the court approves an adoption taking place, the adoptive parent or parents and the child they have adopted become part of the same legal family. The law will treat the child as if he or she is the 'real' child of the adoptive parents, for example in relation to taking their family name, or inheriting from them. Unlike a care order (see Chapter 6) an adoption order cannot be revoked once made; it is a final and permanent severing of the ties between natural parent and child.

All the rights of the natural parents are transferred to the adoptive parents, so that they now decide where the child will live, who he shall see and so on. Very occasionally the court which makes the adoption order will impose a condition on the adoptive parents, for example that they should allow the natural parents access to the child. This is rare in practice since the overriding purpose of adoption is to make a clean break for the child from the past and make a fresh start with a new family.

On what grounds will the court agree to making an adoption order?

The guiding principle for the court is the best interests of the child. In adoption cases, the court will take particular note of the long-term best interests of the child, since adoption is a decision for life. They may feel, for example, that the short-term distress caused by removing a child from his natural parent will be outweighed in the long term by the stability of the adoptive family. Alternatively, it may be argued that the problems of the natural parent who is at present unable to care for the child are short-term and that adoption is inappropriate.

The court will ask some extra questions about whether it is appropriate for the child to be adopted where the application to adopt comes from members of the child's family (related by blood or marriage and in particular where the application is from a natural parent and a step-parent) (see below).

A. QUESTIONS FOR PROSPECTIVE ADOPTERS

Who can be adopted?
Anyone over the age of 19 weeks and under the age of 18 years can be adopted. However, most adoptions are not approved until the child is around a year old (see below).

Who can adopt?
Any adult over the age of 21, either as a single person or as a couple. The only exception to this is where one of those applying to adopt is the child's natural parent (for example, where the prospective adopters are the child's mother and her new partner). Then the natural parent need be only 18 years old so long as her partner is 21 or over.

To be able to adopt jointly as a couple you must be married. Therefore, adoptions by unmarried couples living together, such as gay couples or other co-habitees, can only be approved in the name of one partner. The other partner will have no legal rights in relation to the child.

But surely not just anyone can adopt?
No. All prospective adoptive parents (whether or not they have fostered the child already, or even if they are relatives of the child) are 'screened' by the local authority or the adoption agency through which they apply. The local authority will conduct a 'home study visit' to assess the suitability of the home and the individuals. They will look at such things as whether there are any other children already in the family, and, if so, whether they are

properly clothed, fed and well cared for and whether the home is comfortable, well heated and adequately furnished. If the prospective adopters are a married couple, the local authority will be concerned to ensure that their marriage is a happy and stable one, or, if the applicant is a single person, whether he or she is stable, mature and responsible.

Different authorities carry out these and similar investigations in different ways. In some areas, the home study visit will consist of a number of visits by a social worker. In others, prospective adoptive parents are asked to undertake professional counselling in order that their suitability may be further assessed. If the investigations appear to be intrusive, remember that it is vital that the right decisions are made by the authorities who will almost always have current parental responsibility for the child concerned.

Some authorities have a policy of only permitting the adoption of children by families from the same racial or ethnic background.

What about adoptions by relatives of the child?

There is nothing to prevent a relative of the child applying to adopt him or her. Where for example a child's parent or parents have died, or are unable to take care of him or her properly, the child may go to live with another member of the family, for example the mother's sister. Relatives are defined as anyone related to the child by blood or marriage.

The same rules about the age of the child, the age of the adopters, and the requirement for local authority assessment (above) apply to adoption by relatives. In addition, the court asked to make the adoption order will consider whether it might not be more appropriate to make an order giving temporary rather than permanent rights to the adults caring for the child, in case the natural parents can take over care of the child again in the future.

Often it will seem unnecessary to formalize a new family arrangement made between relatives by making an adoption order. In other cases, especially if the child is very young and there is no prospect at all of the natural parents being able to resume care in the future, it may be appropriate to make it clear in the eyes of the law that this child is now to be treated as, say, his or her aunt's own child, a permanent member of her family.

What about adoptions by step-parents?

Another instance where adoption may be felt to be important to the child's future is where one parent, usually the child's mother, remarries and her new husband wants to establish his rights as legal parent to the child. To do this he must apply jointly with his wife to adopt her child. There may be a number of reasons for doing this – for example, that the family wishes to emigrate and the child's natural father is objecting, or where the natural father is insisting on continued contact which is felt to be against the child's best interests.

The courts are often reluctant to make an adoption order in favour of a step-parent where the natural parent objects, because adoption is a final and permanent severing of birth ties. On the other hand, where the natural parent is no longer in contact with the child, and especially where the child is very young, the courts will be more sympathetic to the idea of allowing a step-parent to adopt if, in the circumstances, making a custody (or 'residence') order in favour of the step-parent would not go far enough (as in the example given above where the family wished to emigrate and the natural father retains the right to object).

A similar reluctance to approve adoptions is apparent where the child was born originally to an unmarried couple, and now one parent has married someone else who wants to share legal rights to the child and hence is seeking to adopt (see below).

Who can arrange an adoption?

Either the Adoption Service run by your local authority (every authority is obliged by law to operate an Adoption Service) or an approved adoption agency. Adoption agencies must be registered and meet conditions laid down by the Secretary of State.

Many agencies have a particular religious or welfare origin and may impose their own conditions on applicants (in addition to the local authority screening process which comes later). If you think that the conditions being imposed are unfair and unjustified you can complain to the Secretary of State, or to your local authority Adoption Service who may then complain on your behalf.

People wanting to adopt babies, at least those without any sort of handicap, now far outnumber the babies available for adoption. More and more unmarried women who once offered their babies for adoption now raise them themselves. This level of demand may be used to justify the imposition of, for example, upper age limits on prospective adopters. So you must expect that even if you can comply with the conditions imposed by an agency getting yourself on to its books may only be the start of a long wait. It should be pointed out that every local Adoption Service has older children looking for adoptive families, possibly with mental or physical handicaps or behavioural problems.

Before the Adoption Service or an adoption agency may apply for an adoption order, the child concerned must be at least 19 weeks old and have lived with the prospective adopters for at least the past 13 weeks. If the original placement was made without a view to adoption, for example if it was originally arranged by the local authority but intended as a fostering placement, or if it was an informal 'private' fostering arrangement by a non-relative of the child, then the child must have lived for at least 12 months with the prospective adopters before an order can be applied for. Private fostering arrangements made with relatives need only satisfy the shorter time periods, of 19 and 13 weeks (see above).

All adoption placements where the prospective adopters are not related to the child must be arranged by the Adoption Service or by a registered agency. Private arrangements by non-relatives, with or without the exchange of money which is prohibited in *all* adoption arrangements, are breaking the criminal law and may be punished by a fine or imprisonment.

I have been fostering a child for the past five years whom I now want to adopt. How do I go about this and might the child be removed in the meantime if his mother objects?

Local authority foster parents have an obligation to keep to the terms of the fostering 'contract' they agree with the authority. When a child is in care, the foster parents have no legal rights to the child and he or she may be removed at any time either by the parents if the child is in voluntary care, or by the authority if the child is in full care and the authority is his legal 'parent' (see Chapter 6).

If as a long-term foster parent you decide that you want to adopt your foster child, you must first obtain the permission of the local authority. You will be unlikely, in practice, to obtain an adoption order if the local authority opposes your application.

If the authority is agreeable, you will be advised to make a formal application for adoption and begin the process of home study visits and so on. It will of course be necessary to secure the consent of the child's natural parent (or parents where the child was born within a marriage) to the adoption going ahead, and if you have been a long-term foster parent for this child you will presumably have a good idea whether or not consent will be forthcoming.

If the parent refuses consent, the court may in special circumstances be prepared to authorize the adoption, if they are convinced that this step is in the child's best interests (see below). If the parent objects and asks for the immediate return of her child, you do at least have the security of knowing that the child cannot be removed from your home for the 3 months which precede the hearing of the adoption application by a court. This is because, once you have started your application to adopt, the child you are hoping to adopt becomes known as 'a protected child' in law. The child will only be protected in this way against removal from your home if he has already lived with you for five years or more.

Will I have to hire a solicitor?

It is probably best if you are advised in the legal procedures surrounding adoption and ultimately represented in court by a solicitor who is practised in dealing with adoption cases. This is especially important if there is any possibility of a dispute over the adoption going ahead (for example where the natural parents will not give their consent or where they have changed their mind in the past). If you are applying to adopt a child whom you have been fostering for a local authority, the authority may offer the services of their own solicitors. Ask your social worker.

See also Chapter 10; 'Getting Legal Advice and Assistance'.

Where will the adoption hearing take place?

The hearing may take place in either your local magistrates' court, county court or in a very few cases, the High Court in London. You should ask your solicitor where the hearing will take place and in which court.

What alternative orders might the court make if it is not convinced that adoption is appropriate at this time?

Under the present law the court may decide instead to make an order for custody – for example, joint custody where a natural parent and a step-parent are applying to adopt (see above and see Chapter 4 for a discussion of the meaning of custody), or an order for custodianship which gives the would-be adopters some, but not all, the rights and duties of legal parents. Both these orders can be changed at some future time if circumstances change, so there is no permanent severing of legal ties between the child and his natural parent(s).

Custodianship has been used to give foster parents, who otherwise have no legal rights and could be asked to give the foster child up at any time, some degree of security; for example, once foster parents have been made custodians, the child cannot be removed without their consent since they take over the right to legal custody. The child's natural parents retain their rights as the administrators of the child's property, to determine his or her religion, to agree to his or her adoption and so on. Custodianship will disappear once the Children Act comes into effect.

Under the Children Act, the court will consider whether it is more appropriate to make a residence or contact order (see Chapter 4) in favour of the would-be adopters, rather than taking the irrevocable step of authorizing adoption (see below).

I am not sure that I am ready to consider adoption, but I would like to feel more secure about the future of our foster child in our family. What could I do?

Under the existing law, one less drastic alternative to adoption is to apply for custodianship (see above). Once the Children Act is in force, you could ask the court for a residence order to be made in your favour. This will mean that the law recognizes that your foster child should live with you and cannot be removed without your permission. You will effectively share all other parental rights and duties with your foster child's natural parents.

I took a short-term foster child into my home last year whom I would now like to adopt. My social worker tells me that he is already 'freed for adoption'. What does that mean?

Where a child has been in care for a number of years and a decision has been taken that it is in the child's best interests to find him a new adoptive family, the child may be 'freed' for adoption before any particular prospective adopters have been found in order that the adoption process can be relatively straightforward once suitable adopters have been found. Effectively the court will have already considered all the issues which arise in relation to making an order for adoption, including the child's best interests, and the agreement of the natural parent(s).

An order made by a court 'freeing' a child for adoption goes through all the formal steps and asks all the same questions as a court would on the application for adoption by a specific person or persons. The agreement of the natural parent(s) must be given at this stage (or dispensed with – see below). The only differences between the 'freeing' procedure and the 'ordinary' adoption procedure are that:

(a) there are no actual adopters yet in mind; and

(b) the order may be revoked, on the application of the natural parent, if the local authority has not found adoptive parents for the child within 12 months.

Freeing orders may be sought by either the local Adoption Service or by an approved agency on behalf of a child on their books. In your case, the local authority has parent.

already freed the child for adoption and therefore your own application to adopt him should be straightforward providing the authority consider you to be a suitable adoptive parent.

B. QUESTIONS FOR NATURAL PARENTS

My child has been in the full care of the local authority for some years now. Can the social workers go ahead and arrange for his adoption without my permission?
No. However long your child has been in full care, the one parental right which you may still assert is your right to consent to or refuse the child's adoption.

In exceptional circumstances the court has the power to decide that your consent should be dispensed with and to allow the adoption to proceed, where the court judges this to be in your child's best interests. This is unlikely to happen where you have maintained contact with your child and certainly not when there is any chance of your child eventually returning home to live with you.

Nevertheless circumstances may exist which convince the court that in the child's long-term interests an adoption order is the best course. Where the court does decide to go ahead with the adoption without parental consent, they must show one of the following:

(a) that you as the child's parent are 'unreasonably withholding consent'. This does not exclude you from arguing against what the social workers think is best for your child. To show the court that you are behaving 'reasonably' and prevent them from dispensing with your consent under this heading, you must explain your reasons for opposing the adoption application and what other plans you have for your child's future; or

(b) that you have failed in your 'parental duties'

towards your child, that is that you have failed to give him or her necessary material and emotional care and support. To justify dispensing with your consent under this heading, it must be shown that you have failed 'without reasonable cause' (for example, an illness or breakdown would be 'reasonable cause') and that your lack of care has lasted for some time; or

(c) that you have abandoned, neglected or ill-treated your child; or

(d) that you are incapable (due to a mental disorder) of giving your consent.

If your consent to adoption is dispensed with on one of the above grounds, you may appeal to the High Court.

What if I gave my consent when adoption was first suggested, but have now changed my mind?

You cannot be asked to consent to adoption until your child is at least six weeks old. If you later have second thoughts, you are free to change your mind at any point up to the court hearing. You will have to explain to the court why you have changed your mind and what new circumstances have arisen since you originally gave your consent which lead you to believe that you can now hope for rehabilitation with your child at some future date. If you cannot do this, or if you change your mind more than once, it may be argued in court that you are 'unreasonably withholding consent' (see above).

The social worker has asked me to agree to 'freeing' my child for adoption. What does this mean?

The social worker and anyone else involved in your child's case will have decided that adoption is in your child's long-term interests. It is unlikely that any specific adoptive parents are in mind at this time, but the authority want to be able to search for a suitable family who can then adopt your child with the minimum of formalities.

If you agree to your child being 'freed' for adoption you are effectively agreeing to give the local authority the right to find adoptive parents for him or her within the next 12 months. If a suitable family is located within 12 months, the only way you will be able to resist the adoption taking place will be to go to the court and tell them that you have changed your mind (see above). So this decision, once made, is as binding on you as a decision to agree to a particular set of adoptive parents. You may apply to revoke the freeing order after 12 months if no adoptive family has been found. It is very important, though, that you do not count on this happening, and should only give your agreement to a 'freeing' order after very careful consideration. Ask your social worker to explain fully to you the implications of giving your agreement to freeing.

If my child is adopted, will I be able to continue to see him?

This will depend on two things. First, whether at the time the court made the adoption order an order allowing you continued access was attached. This is only done in exceptional circumstances where you and your solicitor have made out a very good case for your continuing to have access to your child, and where it is judged to be in his or her best interests.

Otherwise, you may be able to come to some arrangement with your child's adoptive parents giving you continued contact. Once the order has been made, they become in law the child's parents and do not have any obligation to allow you access. They may feel that it would be better for your child to begin afresh and resist continued contact. They should provide you with regular progress reports on your child, but they are not obliged to do any more than this.

I am the father of my ex-girlfriend's child. She is intending to place the baby for adoption. Can I oppose this?

Where a child is born outside marriage, the biological father has no automatic legal rights to the child (see Chapter 4). This means that in the absence of any orders giving parental rights to the father (see below) only the mother is required to give her consent.

Under the provisions of the Family Law Reform Act 1987, which came into effect in April 1989, a court considering making an adoption order on an illegitimate child is now bound to consider whether the father would be likely to apply for an order giving him sole or joint rights with the mother (see Chapter 4), and if so if he is likely to be successful in such an application. The effect of this provision is that the court must consider the possibility of care being provided by the putative father, if this is being offered, as an alternative to adoption by a new family.

If you have maintained regular contact with the child and go to court and put your objections forward, the court may decide not to approve the adoption order. This is only really likely to happen where you have an alternative plan to care for the child yourself, in the absence of the child's mother. It will mean that you will have to return to court to seek either sole or joint parental rights to the child.

If you already have a 'joint parental responsibilities' order (see Chapter 4), you will have the same rights as the child's natural mother to consent to or refuse adoption for your child.

C. QUESTIONS FOR ADOPTED CHILDREN

What difference will my views make on whether the adoption goes ahead?

Your views must be taken into account, both by your social worker and by the court. Obviously if you are set against being adopted, it would be impracticable for the court to make such an order. Your age and apparent maturity will, practically speaking, determine how much notice is taken of your views. If you feel strongly one way or another, talk to your social worker first and discuss how you can tell the court about your feelings.

I am adopted and my adoptive parents have other children of their own living at home. Are they my brothers and sisters?

Yes. Once you have been adopted, your adoptive parents become your mother and father in the eyes of the law and their children are your brothers and sisters. The purpose of adoption is to make you the same as the other children in the family, as much a part of their family as those who were born into it.

Can I find out who my natural parents are?

Yes. If you were adopted as a baby, or have no recollection of your natural parents and want to find out about them, you have the right to see your original birth certificate once you reach the age of 18. It is your choice.

If you were adopted before November 1975, you will be asked to see a counsellor before the details of your original birth certificate are revealed to you. If you were adopted after November 1975 you still have the right to ask for, and be provided with, professional counselling. This is your right, and it may be helpful to talk through the implications of tracing your natural parents with someone experienced in these matters.

The Children Act sets up an Adoption Contact Register, which will consist of a register of adopted persons and a register of relatives of adopted people, where in each case the individuals ask to be placed on the register. It is hoped that this will enable adopted people to contact their natural families more easily.

9: Other Issues Affecting Children and Young People

1. Medical Treatment

The law requires that all forms of medical intervention and treatment – from the most complicated surgery to the simple prescription of drugs – are only undertaken with the consent of the patient. In many cases this consent is implicit, that is, it is assumed so long as the patient does not actually object. In other cases it is difficult for the patient to understand enough about the treatment they are being given to give a fully informed consent. None the less, the general principle which underlies all forms of medical intervention is that it can only be carried out lawfully if the patient consents. Otherwise it is an assault.

At what age can I give my consent to medical treatment?

Where children are concerned, the law states clearly that after the age of 16 a young person may consent to his or her own medical treatment without consulting or getting permission from his or her parents. From 16 onwards, the law regards young people as having the legal 'capacity' to make decisions about medical treatment.

Hospitals and doctors still often consult parents about medical treatment for their children and ask for their agreement, even after their child has turned 16. They may do this as a matter of procedure, or 'good practice' where it is considered important that the parent is kept fully informed and involved. However, the law does not require them to do so and if you do not want your parents involved or even told about your medical treatment, then you have a right to insist that these details are kept private from them – as much a right as they have to ask for details of their own medical history to be kept private from you.

For example, if you are 16 or over and want to receive contraceptive advice and treatment from a doctor, or have a termination of pregnancy at a hospital or clinic, or be prescribed a heroin substitute by your doctor or a drug rehabilitation clinic, you can if you wish tell the person who treats you that you do not want your parents to know that you are receiving treatment or to discuss your case with them at all, and they are bound to maintain that confidentiality.

What if I am under 16?
The law regarding medical treatment of children and young people under 16 is less clear. At one time it was thought that in every case a doctor or any other medical staff treating someone under 16 was obliged by the law to obtain consent from his or her parents who would therefore of course be fully informed about the nature of the treatment.

However, since the decision in the *Gillick* case in 1985, the position appears to depend upon the circumstances of the individual case. In that case, the final judgement from the House of Lords rejected Mrs Gillick's argument that she had a right to be consulted about any contraceptive advice or treatment given to her daughters under the age of 16. Instead they said that if an individual doctor considered a young woman under the age of 16 who came to him or her for contraceptive treatment (or abortion referral) to be sufficiently mature to be able to make this decision without involving her parents, then that doctor could in those circumstances go ahead and treat the young woman on the basis of her own, and not her parents', consent. The details of her case could thereby be kept confidential from her parents, if that was what she wanted.

Can I get contraceptive advice or treatment or an abortion without my parents' consent and without them having to know?

Yes, depending upon how you impress the doctor you go to for help and the doctor's own attitude towards helping you without involving your parents. Inevitably some doctors and clinics are likely to be more sympathetic than others to treating girls under the age of 16 without their parents' consent. All doctors will encourage a girl of this age to talk to her parents if that is possible before seeking treatment. However, if that seems unlikely the law does now allow a doctor to go ahead and treat you on a confidential basis.

If you are worried about finding a doctor who is likely to agree to treat you in confidence, you could consult the Brook Advisory Centre (contraceptive advice and information for young people; see Chapter 10 for full address).

What about other sorts of medical treatment, like being prescribed a drug substitute to break my heroin addiction?

The principle decided in the Gillick case, that a doctor may judge each case on its individual merits, applies in every area of medical treatment. So, if you want to be prescribed a drug substitute to help you to give up an illegal addictive drug, or be referred in confidence to a drugs or alcohol rehabilitation centre, or have any other sort of tests or treatment which you don't want your parents to know about, this will depend once again upon the impression you make on the doctor you go to for help and your reasons for wanting to keep your treatment confidential.

2. Young People and Sexuality

One of the legal problems which gave rise to the Gillick case (see above and introduction) was that the law does not regard a girl under the age of 16 as having the legal 'capacity' to consent to full sexual intercourse.

Therefore any act of intercourse between a girl under 16 and a man or boy of whatever age means that a criminal offence has been committed by the man (but not the girl). This is the case even if the girl has consented to intercourse, or has pretended to the man that she is older than 16. This rule is justified on the basis that it operates to protect young girls by criminalizing the behaviour of any man who has intercourse with her before she has reached the age of 16.

My boyfriend, who is 17, and I have been having sexual intercourse together since I was 14. Does this mean that he could be taken to court?
Yes, he is breaking the law by having intercourse with you while you are still under 16. However, prosecutions are generally only brought where it appears to the police or the authorities that the young woman concerned is being exploited by an older man (even though she may have consented) or has been forced to have intercourse against her will. In your case there is no reason for the authorities to intervene unless it is believed that your boyfriend is exploiting you (which he would be, for example, if he was selling your body to other men) or damaging you either emotionally or physically, for example by infecting you with a venereal disease. If your relationship is a genuine and loving one and there is no element of harm or exploitation, then it is unlikely that the police will prosecute although the offence has been committed.

My friend says that if I have intercourse under age with my boyfriend I will be taken into care. Is this true?
Again this will depend upon the nature of your relationship. If your behaviour is openly promiscuous, for

example if you 'sleep around' with a number of men or if your boyfriend is much older than you and considered to have a damaging influence on you, the present law does allow the local authority to apply to take you into care on the grounds of 'moral danger' (see Chapter 6). However, if this is an exclusive and loving relationship, this is unlikely to happen.

What about boys?
The age of consent for boys is 14. However no criminal offence is committed when a woman has intercourse with a boy under 14.

An offence is committed however if a man has sexual relations with a boy under the age of 21, this time by both parties. After 21, sexual relations between men are lawful only when they take place in a private place, which means that any sexual act which takes place, for example, in a public lavatory, is illegal. Soliciting for sex in a public place is also illegal.

Are sexual relations between members of the same family (for example a father with his daughter) against the law?
Certain sexual relationships are illegal whether or not the parties are adults and consent. The crime of incest is committed if a man has intercourse with his daughter, granddaughter, mother or sister, or a woman with her son, grandson, father or brother. Prosecutions are rare but can happen. Nowadays there is much more awareness of sexual abuse of children (and adults) and a number of organizations can offer counselling and other help on a confidential basis (see Chapter 10). Obviously, as previously noted, if the sexual relationship is with a girl under 16 or is without her consent then this relationship is also illegal on the grounds noted above or because it amounts to rape.

3. Parental Physical Punishment

The law allows parents to use physical punishment on their children and affords them the special protection of the defence of 'reasonable chastisement'. This means that for a parent of a child to be successfully prosecuted for an assault on his child there must be evidence that the severity of the injuries takes the assault beyond 'reasonable chastisement'. In practice, what this means is that the police are reluctant to become involved in cases where parents are alleged to have assaulted their children, or to prosecute parents who ill-treat their children, except where there is evidence of serious harm or injury being suffered as a consequence.

4. Running Away From Home

It is a criminal offence for anyone to help or to harbour a child under the age of 16 who has either run away from their family home or has absconded from the care of a local authority. Although this provision is rarely enforced in practice, and then only by a fine, it makes the operation of 'safe houses' for young runaways unlawful. However, such 'safe houses' where young runaways can get a meal and a bed do operate in some major cities.

No offence is committed by the child or young person who runs away from home or absconds from local authority care, although as we have seen a persistent runaway from local authority care may be placed in 'secure accommodation' as a consequence (see Chapter 5).

5. Driving

The law allows a young person to hold a provisional licence and to learn to drive a car and take a driving test from the age of 17. You can drive a motor bike (with a provisional licence) from the age of 16.

6. Drinking

Children are allowed into public houses licensed to sell alcohol from the age of 14, so long as they are accompanied by an adult. Admission below the age of 14 is at the landlord's discretion and some pubs have special 'family rooms' to allow adult customers to bring their young children with them.

You have the right to ask to be served with an alcoholic drink from the age of 18. The landlord may still refuse you service if he believes that you are under 18. You may be asked to prove your age by showing some personal identification which states your age and includes a photograph. If you say that you are 18 when you are not, and the landlord can show that it was reasonable for him to believe you, then the legal responsibility for buying alcohol under age falls on you.

10: Getting Legal Advice and Representation

The aim of this book is to cover the issues which can arise in relation to children and their rights in law rather than to turn you into a 'do-it-yourself' lawyer. You may feel after looking at this book that you need to talk to a solicitor who can relate the law to your particular problem. If so, you should first contact your local Citizens' Advice Bureau or Law Centre and explain your problem briefly to them. They may suggest that you make an appointment and discuss the problem with them, or they may refer you to a local solicitor whom they can recommend. Ask to be referred to a solicitor who is experienced in handling cases involving children or families. You could also contact one of the addresses given below for help and advice.

You may be anxious about how much legal advice will cost you. The Citizens' Advice Bureau or Law Centre should refer you to a solicitor who participates in the Legal Aid scheme. This means that the first interview should be at a 'fixed fee' and for further work you can apply for legal aid to pay towards the full cost. You will be asked to fill out a form giving details of your income and savings and on the basis of these figures a decision will be made whether or not you will qualify for legal aid.

It used to be the case that legal aid assessment for a child less than 16 years old was based upon his parents' means. Now, if legal action is brought by or on behalf of a young person of whatever age, even if he or she may still be living with his or her parents, assessment for the purposes of legal aid is based on the young person's own independent means.

Useful addresses (in alphabetical order)
Advisory Centre for Education,
18 Victoria Park Square,
London E2.
For advice on education rights.

Brook Advisory Centres,
Head Office, 233 Tottenham Court Road,
London W1.
For advice on contraception.

Centre for Integration Studies in Education,
4th Floor, 415 Edgeware Road,
London NW2.
For advice on integrated special needs education.

Childline,
Faraday Building,
Addle Hill,
London EC4.
Telephone: (01)-236 2380.
Counselling and help for children who have been physi-
cally or sexually abused. A telephone contact service.

Child Poverty Action Group,
1–5 Bath Street,
London EC1V 9PY.
For advice on welfare benefits.

Children's Legal Centre,
20 Compton Terrace,
London N1.
For advice on all aspects of children's rights.

EPOCH (End Physical Punishment of Children),
77 Holloway Road,
London N7.
For advice on preventing the physical punishment of children.
Physical punishment by teachers is monitored by the Childrens Legal Centre (above).

Family Rights Group,
6 Manor Gardens,
London N7.
For advice on custody and access disputes and other family disputes.

National Association of Young People in Care,
20 Compton Terrace,
London N1.
For children who are, or have been, in care.

Release,
169 Commercial Road,
London E1.
For advice on legal aspects of drug usage.

Trade Union Congress
Organization and Industrial Relations Dept.,
Great Russell Street,
London WC1.
For advice on YTS and youth employment rights.

Notes

Notes

Notes